Digging for Buried Treasure 2:

52 More Prop-Based Play Therapy Interventions For Treating the Problems of Childhood

Written by:
Paris Goodyear-Brown, LCSW, RPT-S

Resources and upcoming workshop information can be found at
www.parisandme.com.
For supervision, consultation or training, send e-mail to
paris@parisandme.com *or contact by phone at **615-397-9480***.

Dedication:

For Sam and Madison, who provide me with shocking degrees of joy and laughter every day and for my husband, the co-creator of our family narrative and my constant cheerleader. My cup runneth over.

Digging for Buried Treasure 2: 52 More Prop-Based Play Therapy Interventions for Treating the Problems of Childhood

Copyright 2005 by Paris Goodyear-Brown

All rights reserved. No portion of this book may be reproduced, stored in a retrieval system, or transmitted in any form or by any means: electronic, mechanical, photocopy, recording, or any other, except for brief quotations in printed review, without the prior permission of the author.

ISBN: 1-59744-035-3

Table of Contents

Table of Contents..**1-4**

Introduction..**5-7**

Tools for Use in Treatment Planning............**8**
    How Far Can You See?..9-12
    Step-by-Step..13-15
    Wishing Well...16-18
    What's on the Other Side...19-21
    Edible Wishing Wands...22-25
    Throw it A-Weigh..26-28

Building Safety and Support with Traumatized Clients..**29**
    No Place Like Home..30-33
    Learning to Bear It...34-37
    Crowning Community..38-40
    Personalized Pinwheels..41-44

© Paris Goodyear-Brown, 2005. All Rights Reserved.

Empowerment Exercises for Traumatized Clients 45
- Megaphones to Make a Point 46-49
- Blow the Whistle On 'Em 50-53
- Door Hangers 54-57
- Keep Your Hands Off Me 58-61
- Puppet on a String 62-65

Sensory Processing Exercises for Trauma Survivors 66
- See No Evil, Hear No Evil 67-70
- Monster Ears 71-74
- Putting the Pieces Together 75-78
- Pieces and Parts 79-82

Skill Building (Feelings Identification, Anger Management, Impulse Control, Pro-social Skills) 83
- Taking Your Temperature 84-87
- Inside/ Outside Feelings 88-91
- Pens Up!! Switch! Draw!! 92-95
- Extinguish the Behavior 96-98
- Mad Maracas 99-102
- Fire Breathing Dragons 103-106
- Ants in Your Pants 107-110
- On The Other Hand 111-114
- What's Bugging You? 115-118
- Treat 'Em with Kid Gloves 119-122

Exercises for Building Self-Esteem 123
Fingerprint Friends 124-126
Sandtray Circles 127-130
Don't Put All Your Eggs in One Basket 131-134
Geodes 135-137
Under Attack!! 138-140
Putting a Positive Spin on It 141-144

Cognitive-Behavioral Play Therapy Techniques 145
Punching Holes in That Theory 146-148
Lasso the Loser 149-151
The Why Wheel 152-155
Thinking Caps 156-159
Erase the Place 160-162
Clearing the Clouds Away 163-166

Activities to Strengthen the Attachment Relationship 167
Sweet Dreams Lotion Potion 168-171
Shaving with Dad 172-175
Meet in the Middle 176-178
The Toddler Tale 179-181
Powder Prints 182-184
"You're a Star" 185-187

© Paris Goodyear-Brown, 2005. All Rights Reserved.

Termination Activities: Saying Goodbye 188
    Bandage Banners 189-192
    Calendar Collage 193-195
    Graduation Gear 196-199
    Pat on the Back 200-202
    Termination Take-Aways 203-205

References and Resources 206-208

Introduction

This second volume of *Digging for Buried Treasure* was another labor of love. It was written in direct response to the stated needs of clinicians who have approached me in my travels. Many of the interventions that I describe and model in my workshops for treating traumatized children are encapsulated in this manual. In this volume, techniques for helping traumatized children to feel safer and more secure are addressed, as well as empowerment exercises and interventions that target the somatosensory integration of traumatic memories. Another area that professionals have requested is more help with treatment planning. Therefore, a chapter of the book is dedicated to these activities. I have also heard repeatedly that clinicians need more practical interventions to help families with attachment issues. A whole chapter is devoted to exercises aimed at changing the quality of the attachment bond. Clinicians who found the skill building exercises in Volume I helpful have requested more. The skill building activities in this book cover emotional literacy, anger management, impulse control and pro-social interactions. Lastly, a chapter is devoted to termination activities because creating a meaningful "goodbye" for clients is necessary for concretizing all the therapeutic work that has come before. Once again, I want to make it clear that the children and families with whom I work are the real authors of this volume. It is because of their courage, creativity, willing to risk, and deep desire to heal that the techniques in this book have evolved.

I have labeled the techniques in this book "prop-based" because each technique utilizes a prop of some sort. I have found the use of concrete items in treatment to be invaluable. The props serve several functions. First and most importantly, props serve to break through the resistance of child clients. They often come to therapy believing that they are going to have to "talk" or "perform". When a prop is placed in their hands, the worry of having to talk the whole session is alleviated. The introduction of the object also gives the child an excuse to break eye contact which can be intimidating during the initial relationship bulding phase of treatment. Second, the prop often serves to concretize or carries a metaphoric message related to a concept such as anger or fear and allows for work to be done consciously and unconsciously at the same time. Third, the props often serve as a vehicle for externalizing a problem or issue that the child is facing. Once the problem has been put outside the child, the child is better equipped to analyze the situation and to generate solutions or coping strategies to deal with it.

© Paris Goodyear-Brown, 2005. All Rights Reserved.

Fourth, research into neurolinguistics tells us that children have different learning styles (auditory, visual, kinesthetic, or a combination of these). Using props allows for kinesthetic learning to occur and can augment visual and auditory processes that are taking place in the playroom. Finally, it's just plain fun to play with props! Children can work on even the most difficult problems while having a parallel experience that naturally creates enjoyment.

Many therapists have natural gifts for working with children. Creating new play therapy activities comes easily to many. Others prefer to use previously created interventions from books and spend their energies molding the exercises to their client populations. Please let me stress that no intervention should ever be pulled out of a hat or even this book without giving careful consideration to the client's needs, the treatment goals and the placement of the intervention in the continuum of the therapeutic process. For you creative types, this book will likely spark a whole new batch of your own interventions. For those of you who call yourself "creatively challenged", you will adapt these techniques to your own special way of interacting with children. For all of you, the techniques are broken down into sub-sections for easy reference.

Treatment Modality: This section gives you a quick glance at the treatment settings in which the technique might be most appropriate. Some techniques are more suited for work with individuals while others are more appropriate for group or family work. Most of the techniques could be modified to work in any of these treatment milieues.

Population: The age range of who may benefit from the intervention is listed here. Be aware that the developmental age is a more relevant guide than chronological age.

Treatment Phase: This section helps you to place the intervention within the therapeutic process. These stages are loosely broken down into the initial or joining phase in which a relationship is being built and trust is being established; the middle or working phase in which the meat of treatment is occurring; and the termination or ending phase of treatment in which previous work is being integrated and clients are saying goodbye.

Props: This section details the materials that you will need to complete each activity.

© Paris Goodyear-Brown, 2005. All Rights Reserved.

Procedure: This section gives a step by step guide for the clinician detailing how to orchestrate the intervention.

Processing Questions: This section lists questions that the clinician may use to process the intervention after it is complete and to deepen the client's awareness or therapeutic learning.

Homework assignment: This section gives a homework assignment for the client. The homework helps crystallize new concepts, practice new skills and gain new experiences that strengthen the therapeutic work being done in session. Homework assigments may need to be modified according to the age and capacities of the child.

Special considerations: This section will sometimes describe populations with which the intervention may be more or less effective, adaptations to be made for children with various challenges and general "watch outs" that have grown out of this therapist's repeated completion of these interventions with clients.

Applications and modifications: This section often delineates alternative settings in which the intervention can be used. If the procedures described above were geared for work with an individual client, this section may discuss ways in which the technique can be modified for use in groups.

Many clinicians have asked how I generate these ideas. The answer is not complicated. I let the prop guide me. I ask myself how a particular tool could be helpful in communicating a therapeutic metaphor or teaching a therapeutic skill. I ask myself, "For what function does this object exist?" For a set of magnifying glasses, the answer is "to magnify things...to make certain images larger". Then I ask myself what parts of a child's life need to be magnified. Most children who come to therapy have low self-esteem and tend to see and hear the negative statements people make about them more clearly than the positive ones. Out of this train of thought came the technique, "Magnifying the Feel Goods". Try the process on your own and soon you'll have a whole new repertoire of interventions. In closing, I would like to address the title of this book. Each child whom we see has inside himself a treasure trove of riches. Many times the child needs help finding these beautiful gems within himself. It is my hope that careful application of the techniques enumerated in this text will result in uncovering the buried treasure within the children we serve.

© Paris Goodyear-Brown, 2005. All Rights Reserved.

Tools for Use in Treatment Planning

How Far Can You See?

Treatment Modality: Individual/Group/Family
Population: Ages 5 to 18
Treatment Phase: Working phase

Treatment Goals:
1. To help the client envision future
2. To assist the client in developing goals
3. To create measurable and specific goals for the treatment plan

Props:
Binoculars (real)
Binoculars (toy)
Spy glass
Paper
Markers/crayons
Old magazines

Procedure:
One of the first jobs faced by a therapist with any new client is goal setting. Clinicians assess the symptoms with which our clients present, arrive at a diagnosis and then create treatment goals. There is a clear correlation in the link

between a client's "ownership" of or investment in goal setting and a positive outcome in treatment. It is necessary for clinicians to work collaboratively with clients to design treatment goals. However, this is often difficult for children. When asked directly what they "need to work on" children will often say "I need to stop fighting" or "No more running away." It can be challenging to help clients restate these goals in positive terms. Part of the challenge is that these children may be stuck in negative behavior patterns. They may be unable to see the possibility of an identity that does not revolve around these negative behaviors. One of the strategies often used when working with adults in the goal setting process is the prompt, "Imagine yourself in five years-what would you want your life to look like?" Children's conception of time is not as clearly developed as adults and their sense of longevity is considerably shorter. Therefore, this activity is meant to help child clients project into the future.

The therapist has at least two different pairs of binoculars available (perhaps one is real, the other a toy, a pair of opera glasses or a spyglass). Let the child choose a large object to focus on. If the playroom has a window, it might be the tree outside the window. The child might choose the sandtray, or a large puppet. Ask the child if he really *needs* the binoculars to see this object. Since you have chosen a large object first, the answer should be no. Then have the child walk over to the shelves or bins and choose one very small item (perhaps a sandtray miniature). Have them put it on a flat surface on the other side of the room. Ask the child if they can see it clearly without the binoculars. The child will usually request the binoculars at this time. Discuss the number of details on the object that can be seen when the binoculars are used. Compare this to long range vision in goal setting. Explain that the miniature is like a goal that may seem unattainable early in treatment, but by taking the long view, or looking ahead, one can see more specifics about how to meet the goal. The child is then invited to draw a tiny picture that describes one of his goals in treatment (an example would be "to sit in my chair for five full minutes"-this is a big goal for some of our ADHD kids). Pin this picture up on the far end of the room. It is hard to see it from that distance, but with the binoculars, goal attainment comes into focus. Allow the child to use the binoculars and also to stand up and take physical steps towards the drawing. With every step forward, the goal gets closer and the child doesn't need the binoculars as much. This can be used as a jumping off point for discussing how our perspective shifts as we work towards our goals. A fun addendum to this activity is to have the child stop with each step and draw another quick picture of one way to work towards this goal. An example follows: Johnny struggles with shyness. Because of this, he has few friends and feels lonely a lot. His first, tiny picture might be of him playing ball with some boys. Johnny takes the binoculars and brings the goal into focus and then takes a physical step forward. He stops here and draws a picture of saying "hello" to a peer or he might just write the word "hi". This is step one towards meeting that goal. Progressive drawings can be completed with each drawing showing a sub-step or sub-stage needed to meet the goal.

Processing Questions:
What do binoculars do?
What is a goal?
What was it like to draw a picture of who you want to become?
How clearly could you see your goal when it was posted all the way across the room?
What changed for you when you were able to use the binoculars?
What is the next step in reaching your goal?

© Paris Goodyear-Brown, 2005. All Rights Reserved.

Homework Assignment:
At the end of the activity, the client should have used the binoculars to help clarify the steps needed to reach the goals in his pictures. Out of this exercise should come the answer to, "What is the next step in reaching your goal?" Design a way of recording the completion of this target behavior (a chart, form, journal, etc.). Ask the child or family to record baseline data around how frequently the child engages in the target behavior (in Johnny's case the first target behavior could be saying hello).

Special Considerations:
The activity involves full body kinesthetic involvement and drawing. Clinicians will want to make sure that the child client is comfortable with both of these forms of expression before attempting the exercise. Also, binoculars can be tricky and it will be helpful to have a quick training lesson with the child on how to bring objects into focus before the goal setting activity begins. This will cut down on frustration and distraction during the actual exercise.

Applications and Modifications:
One way to add an extra dimension to this exercise is to use old magazines and invite the client to cut out pictures and words that describe the goal. Have them make a collage out of these images and tape this to the far wall (as opposed to a simple drawing). The binoculars can then be focused ona particular part of the image and the exercise may proceed as described above. Upon completion of the exercise, all the pictures generated while moving towards the target goal can be packaged together into a goal book for easy reference.

Step by Step

Treatment Modality: Individual/Group/Family
Population: Ages 3 to adult
Treatment Phase: Beginning phase

Treatment Goals:
1. To help the client take ownership of the therapeutic process
2. To help the client concretize therapeutic goals
3. To help the client divide therapeutic goals into discrete, manageable steps

Props:
Clay
Clay cutting tools
A sandtray
Sandtray miniatures

Procedure:
This activity is aimed at helping clients take ownership of their treatment, create vision for the changes that can take place in their relationships, behaviors, self-image, etc and establish goals for achieving these changes. Begin by asking the client to visualize one way in which he wants his life to be different at

© Paris Goodyear-Brown, 2005. All Rights Reserved.

the end of treatment than it is now. Divide the sandtray into halves and invite the client to make a picture of the way he wants his life to be different in the sand. Depending on the age of the client, this may be a concrete representation or may include more abstract, symbolic imagery. Process the completed image with the client. Then introduce the clay and invite the client to help you create a staircase that will go in the other half of the sandtray. Because working with clay is fun and soothing for children., verbal information often flows more freely as the client's hands are busy molding. Have the client cut the clay into blocks of increasing length. These will ultimately be stacked with the longest block on the bottom and the shortest block on top to form a staircase. Help the client specify the long term treatment goal associated with the image he created on the other side of the tray. Explain that this goal will be easier to achieve if it is broken down into steps. Explain that each step helps the client climb closer towards his goal. As each clay block is cut, help the client generate sub-stages of the larger goal and write them into the clay. For example, the long term goal of "worrying less" might be first addressed by having the client become aware of all the things he does worry about. This step in the process would be carved into the longest clay block and placed in the sand. Each successive sub-stage of the goal is carved into each clay step and added to the staircase. When the steps are all delineated, a miniature can be used to "climb" the stairs and stand at the top, overlooking the pictoral image on the other side of the tray. This helps the client understand how good it will feel to see the changes when they are completed.

Processing Questions:
What do you picture when you try to see your life with the changes you hope to achieve?
Choose one change that you hope to achieve. Can you picture this one in detail? Can you recreate it in the sandtray?
What steps will need to be completed to meet this goal?

© Paris Goodyear-Brown, 2005. All Rights Reserved.

How does the changed world look to the miniature who climbed the staircase?

Homework Assignment:
The client may take his personalized staircase home with him. Have the client begin to practice the first step in the process of working towards her treatment goals. This is usually tied to becoming more aware of when, where, how often or in what way a certain behavior, feeling or thought is triggered.

Special Considerations:
Younger clients may have very simple treatment goals, like "to feel better" or "to listen to my teacher". The therapist will have more responsibility for helping these clients delineate the steps that will move them towards their goals. In fact, the youngest children may understand only that the staircase means you move from one place to another. This can serve as a developmentally appropriate explanation of how change happens.

Applications and Modifications:
Clients in a group setting can utilize this goal setting approach, especially when a group has been created to focus on a particular treatment issue (i.e. domestic violence) or to serve a particular population (i.e, children with ADD). The treatment goals and the individual steps needed to achieve the treatment goals will be similar enough in these kinds of groups that all members will benefit from helping to create the step by step guide to change. In a group setting, it would be more valuable to use larger building materials for the staircase, as all group members could be more kinesthetically engaged in the building process.

© Paris Goodyear-Brown, 2005. All Rights Reserved.

Wishing Well

Treatment Modality: Individual/Group/Family
Population: Ages 3 to adult
Treatment Phase: Beginning phase

Treatment Goals:
1. To help the therapist assess the client's wishes and dreams
2. To encourage utilization of the client's internal desires and determination
3. To help the client create a visual image of peace and joy that can become internalized

Props:
Miniature wishing well
Play money
Sandtray
Other sandtray miniatures
Camera

Procedure:

This activity gives clients an opportunity to engage in kinesthetic activity while utilizing their abilities to dream and fantasize. Children love to throw money into pools and fountains. Begin by asking the child if she has ever seen someone throwing money into a fountain as a wish is made. Show the child the wishing well and place it in the center of the sandtray. Give the client a handful of play coins. Tell the client that for each coin she throws into the well, she can make a wish. Make it clear to the client that anything can be wished for, both things possible and things seemingly impossible. The therapist might give a couple of fantastical examples and a couple of practical ones to get the client started. The client is then encouraged to throw the coins and make the wishes out loud. Clients who are older may feel more challenged if they must throw the coins with their eyes closed or from a greater distance. The therapist, as scribe, writes down all of the wishes. Wishes often serve as a door into the treatment goals that a client needs to address. Wishes often speak of desired change in family or peer relationships or desired changes in the self. All of this information is important for the therapist in treatment planning. After the client has exhausted their "wish list", the therapist reads the wishes back to the client. The client is encouraged to choose one of the wishes and actually create a world or picture in the sandtray that reflects this wish fulfilled. For example, if the client wishes for world peace, she could create a world of sandtray miniatures that conveys her image of the world at peace. As the client creates and gazes upon the world of the sandtray, this visual image can become internalized and available for future use as a soothing tool. Take a picture of the completed sandtray and make it available to the client.

Processing Questions:

If you could wish for anything in the world, what would you wish for?

What is one change in your family that you wish would happen? In the world? In your self? In your friendships?

Homework Assignment:

Encourage the client to visualize the sandtray she created at least once a day. Give the client a copy of the wish list and ask the client to decide which of the wishes could actually be addressed in treatment.

Special Considerations:

Clients are likely to generate many fantastical wishes. They will make statements like, "I wish I were a bird" or "I wish I had all the money in the whole world." The path for turning any of these wished into treatment goals may be hidden. In this case, the therapist should explore further with the client. What is it about being a bird that the client envies? If it is freedom, the next question is "freedom from what?" In this way, the underlying area of desired change can be worked into a practical treatment goal.

Applications and Modifications:

One fun modification of this activity is to allow the client, group or family to create their own wishing well from scratch. This can be done with an old box, a cheap bucket, a paper towel role and some string. In a group setting, the wishing well can become a ritualized part of group each week. At the beginning of the group, each member is given a piece of play money and is allowed to make a wish out loud in front of the group. Structure the activity so that the wishes are related to something that they hope will happen during group, some topic they wish to address or some behavior they wish to change as a result of the group experience.

© Paris Goodyear-Brown, 2005. All Rights Reserved.

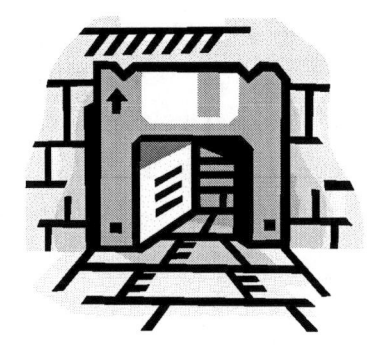

What's on the Other Side?

Treatment Modality: Individual/Group/Family

Population: Ages 6 to adult (particularly helpful with adolescents)

Treatment Phase: Beginning phase

Treatment Goals:
1. To help the client pinpoint needed areas of change
2. To help the client engage in goal setting
3. To help the client prioritize goals
4. To help the client craft a vision of the problem "all better"
5. To positively impact the client's sense of hope

Props:
A freestanding door with casement (Lego and PlayMobile have these) or Clay
A sandtray
Sandtray Miniatures

Procedure:
Children and adolescents often come to treatment because another person, generally a parent or teacher, believes that the child needs help. It can be challenging to help the client take

ownership of the therapeutic process. This activity is a fun way to help children begin to look at how they would like their lives to be different. The sandtray provides the boundary for this intervention. It is a soothing medium that encourages unconscious content to be shared. It allows for kinesthetic involvement, a deepening of mind/body connectedness in treatment, and for the child's own creativity and expressive abilities to take the lead.

Begin by introducing the door props to the client. The door can be as simple as an arched entryway. The therapist then talks to the client about doorways, highlighting how they take you from one view of reality to another. The therapist may contrast the look and feel of the office lobby to the look and feel of the playroom. Remind the client that these two spaces are only separated by a door. Have the client place the door he chooses in the center of the sandtray. On one side of the door, have the client create a sandtray world that depicts "the thing that bothers him the most". When this is completed, have the client create a sandtray world on the other side of the door that depicts the problem "all better". This activity can help the client clarify the changes he wants to make. Have the client choose a miniature to be himself. The client places the self-object in the problem half of the tray and describes how the self feels in this world, what he sees, fears, etc. Then the client moves the self-object through the door and repeats the same perspective taking exercise. Treatment goals stem from questions regarding how the figure opens the door and gets into the new world.

Processing Questions:

What kind of door do you want to make (or choose)?
Think about the thing that bothers you the most. Create a picture of it in the sandtray.
Picture the problem all better. Put this in the sandtray.
What is one small step you can take today to begin to make the problem better?

© Paris Goodyear-Brown, 2005. All Rights Reserved.

Homework Assignment:
After the client has given one step he can take to make the problem better, create a chart to help him track the implementation of this new strategy over the next week. For example, if the client is dealing with social anxiety, the first step may be saying hello to one person each day. A positive reinforcement system can be designed to help the client track the performance of the new behavior while encouraging rewards (by self or caregiver) for said performance.

Special Considerations:
Clients who are stuck in negative externalizing behaviors will often downplay the problems that these cause. They may place the blame for their difficulties outside of themselves. A client may see his little brother as the problem. Therefore, the problem "all better" revolves around change in the brother. It is important for the therapist to gently confront the belief that the client can change anyone else. The client must be helped to see that he only has control over his own choices, behavioral responses, etc.

Applications and Modifications:
It can be very enlightening to use this technique in family therapy. Each family member creates his or her own door and sandtray that characterizes the problem and the problem all better. As each person gives explication of his or her sandtray, the other family members get three dimensional pictures of how the person sees the problem.

Edible Wishing Wands

Treatment Modality: Individual/Group/Family
Population: Ages 3 to 12
Treatment Phase: Assessment/joining phase

Treatment Goals:
1. To give the client an experience of power and control
2. To target problem areas for the client
3. To assess the client's projective wish fulfillment
4. To shape goals based on the above

Props:
Whole wheat bread
Peanut butter
Pretzel wands (8 inches long)
Star shaped cookie cutter
Ribbon

Procedure:

Most clinicians are familiar with the assessment technique that asks the child to list three wishes. Intermittent repetitions of this tool can give the therapist rich projective information related to the client's wish fulfillment fantasies and the resolution of issues. This adaptation of "The Three Wishes" allows each client to create a personalized wand and the best part is it's edible!

Begin by asking the child about magic wands. Where has she seen them before? In what context? What characters in stories, movies, etc. use wands and how do they use them? Wands are a symbol of power and often allow the holder of the wand to make the world more to his or her liking. Tell the client that she is going to make her very own wand-and eventually eat it! Food is one of the first nurturing activities that occurs between infants and primary caregivers. It is one of the first ways that children understand that their needs can be met, that they are loved and safe. Engaging children in the making of food allows them to feel competent while triggering positive attachment behavior. Begin by giving the child two pieces of bread and allowing her to cut out two star shaped pieces. As the child cuts out each star, encourage her to describe two wishes that have come true. These may be as simple as dad coming home from a long trip or getting a dog for her birthday. The next step is to put peanut butter between the two pieces and create a star shaped sandwich. Finally, have the child take one long pretzel stick and embed it in the peanut butter, thereby creating a handle for the wand. Once the wand is finished, invite the client to decorate it with ribbons, etc. Perhaps each ribbon could represent a different wish that the child would like to make. When the wand is complete, invite the child to wave it while stating three wishes out loud. The power of the experience may be augmented by having the client wear a wizard's cloak, hat or even a pair of fairy wings.

© Paris Goodyear-Brown, 2005. All Rights Reserved.

Processing Questions:
What do you think of when you see a magic wand?
What wishes did you make using your wand?
Do you think that your parent/caregiver knows that you wish for these things?
Pick the most important wish. What is one step that you could take to begin to move towards the fulfillment of that wish?

Homework Assignment:
This technique is an assessment tool for the clinician and as such may not always be associated with homework. However, the therapist could ask the child to become aware of times throughout the week when she is wishing for something. Perhaps the client is watching other children play together and wishes she could join. Encourage her to take the first step toward making that dream come true. In the above example, the first step could be walking up and saying hello. Have the child report back next week.

Special Considerations:
Whenever a therapist is considering using a food based intervention, food allergies must be ruled out. Moreover, the role that food already plays in the life of the client will be important to assess. This technique could be contraindicated for children with eating disorders or for children who struggle with obesity. It should also go without saying that the caregiver's permission must be obtained before using food in treatment.

Applications and Modifications:
This technique was originally designed for use in individual sessions, as part of an assessment process. However, making edible wands with a group can be beneficial on a number of levels, particularly as it relates to the universalization of experience. The normalizing function of groups may be

© Paris Goodyear-Brown, 2005. All Rights Reserved.

especially useful, as children realize that the things they wish for (i.e., for their parents to stop fighting, for dad to come home, etc.) are wishes that are shared by their peers.

This technique could also be adapted for trauma survivors. The wand would serve as an instrument of power that distances the survivor from the perpetrator while allowing for wish fulfillment in relation to the perpetrator. In this case, the three wishes could be three things the client wishes she could change about what happened, or three things that the client wishes she could do to the perpetrator. In the book <u>Gabby the Gecko</u> a character named Wiley the Wizard Lizard casts a spell on Gabby. After a journey of discovery and empowerment, in which Gabby finds the way to break the spell of silence that was cast over her, she gets to break the wizard's wand over her knee. After reading this book, a client could make a wand that represents the perpetrator's power and have the full kinesthetic experience of breaking the wand that symbolizes the own abuse over her own knee.

Throw it A-Weigh

Treatment Modality: Individual/Group/Family
Population: Ages 5 to adult
Treatment Phase: Working Phase

Treatment Goals:
1. To help the client set treatment goals
2. To help the client identify what weighty beliefs, feelings, relationships may get in the way of reaching his goals
3. To help the client discard burdens that may slow down his progress in treatment

Props:
A backpack
Rocks of various shapes and sizes or
Rock shaped bouncing balls
Paper
Markers

Procedure:
During the initial phase of treatment, a significant amount of time is spent building rapport and setting goals. This activity is a natural addition to the goal setting process. Most school aged children are familiar with backpacks. Invite the client to

bring in his own backpack or allow him to choose from some in the playroom. Draw a picture of a mountain. Draw a picture of the client at the bottom of the mountain and another with him at the top. Write the treatment goal at the top above the picture of the client. Explain to the client that getting to the top of the mountain (and accomplishing the treatment goal) is a journey. It requires that you take certain things along. Have the client help generate a list of things that would be needed on a trip up the mountain - things that would be packed in the backpack. (These might be items like water, a compass, extra socks, a raincoat, etc.). Then help the client make a list of the faulty beliefs, poor communication skills, negative behaviors, etc. that they carry with them everyday. Explain that each of these things weighs the client down and makes his journey up the mountain harder. Have the client put on the empty backpack. Go back through the list of burdens, and add a large stone to the backpack for each of the weights on the list. Then allow the client to choose which items he still has room for to get him through the journey. As the client realizes that not only are the rocks really heavy, but they take up valuable space needed for his "survival kit", his motivation for removing these burdens will increase. Invite the client to empty out as many of the rocks as necessary to make room for his needed materials. The emptied rocks can form the bulk of issues to be addressed in treatment.

Processing Questions:

How did it feel to imagine yourself at the top of the mountain (attaining your goal)?
How did it feel to have all those rocks in your backpack?
Did you have room for the other things you needed with the rocks in there?
What did you have to do to make room for your survival kit?
How can we help you to begin to get rid of each of these burdens in your own life?

© Paris Goodyear-Brown, 2005. All Rights Reserved.

Homework Assignment:
Ask the client to engage in a visualization exercise each night before bed. The client should visualize himself at the foot of the mountain, deliberately dumping out all the rocks that represent the weights he carries. Then the client should visualize himself repacking the backpack with everything he needs. The client should continue the visualization until he can see himself at the top of the mountain.

Special Considerations:
For this exercise to be beneficial, the client has to be emotionally and psychologically ready to show the therapists the behaviors, beliefs and aspects of relationships that are problematic for him. It is important that the therapist anticipate and normalize some of these for the client.

Applications and Modifications:
After the burdens have been removed, the focus can then be shifted to gathering the survival kit materials to successfully finish the journey. Parallels can be drawn between various pieces of equipment and valuable coping strategies. For example, the traveler would need plenty of water. Water is for drinking and replenishing the body. In the same way, the client may need to replenish himself through social supports or a "diet" of positive self-talk.

Building Safety and Support with Traumatized Clients

No Place Like Home

Treatment Modality: Individual
Population: Ages 5 to 18
Treatment Phase: Working phase

Treatment Goals:
1. To re-establish a sense of safety and security for the client
2. To assist the client in creating or remembering a safe place
3. To help the client envision the safe place while anxious or otherwise escalated
4. To mitigate anxiety caused by trauma by utlizing internalized safety images

Props:
Ruby red slippers (kid's size)
Or an old pair of women's shoes
Red sequins, glitter, etc.
Glue
Or a sandtray and miniature ruby red slipper

© Paris Goodyear-Brown, 2005. All Rights Reserved.

Procedure:

Traditional approaches to relaxation and stress management have focused on visualization and guided imagery techniques. Often the verbal prompt given by the therapist is something like, "visualize one of your safe places". The problem is that many traumatized children have no safe place. For these children, a more helpful prompt would be *"imagine* a safe place", or *"create* a safe place". The aim of this exercise is to stimulate the child's creative process while giving express permission to fantasize about a safe place. The therapist starts by asking if the child has ever seen the movie "The Wizard of Oz". If the child has seen the movie or read the books, then proceed with the exercise. If the child has not been exposed to this movie/book then it is best to talk with their parents to decide if it is an age-appropriate time for them to view the movie.

Engage the child in a discussion of the movie. The little girl, Dorothy, doesn't like her home and wishes to go somewhere else. Have the child describe what she remembers about the land of Oz. Ask the child how she felt at the point in the movie when the film changes from the drab black and white of home to the brilliant colors of Oz. Perhaps make the comparison between drab Kansas and the child's own experience. Present the old pair of shoes and establish the metaphor that these old shoes represent the everyday life of the child (that life might be filled with violence, anxiety, etc.). Then introduce the sequins, glitter, etc. and establish these as representing imagination and the child's creative ability, even magic. Invite the child to create Dorothy's magic slippers by gluing the red glitter, etc. to the shoes. This activity will keep her hands busy while allowing the therapist and the child to engage in a joint attention task, thereby decreasing the child's defensiveness. As the child works on the slippers, invite her to begin verbally describing the safe place she would like to create for herself. She can then draw a picture or create a sandtray in which her safe place is depicted. Invite the child to put on

© Paris Goodyear-Brown, 2005. All Rights Reserved.

the ruby red slippers and close her eyes (some children will not feel safe enough to close their eyes-do not push them to do so.) During this phase of the activity the therapist is helping the child to internalize the safety image that she has created in the sand or on paper. Ask the child to click her heels and picture herself being transported to the safe place. Once the child has practiced internalizing the safety image by clicking her heels together, remind her of the mantra that Dorothy chanted "There's no place like home, There's no place like home." Invite the child to create her own mantra that helps call up the safety image. It might be something like "My safe place, my own". This activity can be repeated as often as the child requests it. Process the feelings that the child experiences while visualizing her created safe place. Generalize the usefulness of these feelings to other environments (home, school, etc) and encourage the child to practice bringing up the internal safety image without the shoes, with their eyes open, etc.

Processing Questions:
How did Dorothy feel in her black and white world at the beginning of the movie?
What was different about her new world (Oz)?
What parts of the world that you created make you feel especially safe?
How can you get to your safe place without clicking your heels?

Homework Assignment:
Once the child has practiced envisioning her safe place in the playroom, give her the task of deliberately calling up this image 3 times between sessions. When the child returns, process what this experience was like.

© Paris Goodyear-Brown, 2005. All Rights Reserved.

Special Considerations:
In the movie, Dorothy closes her eyes before clicking her heels, but this may be a particularly difficult task for traumatized children. Post-traumatic stress symptoms often include hypervigilance, a sense of always having to be alert and "on guard". In a sense, these children are always waiting for the other shoe to drop. Moreover, when these children close their eyes, they may only see violence and horror. Although these children can be invited to close their eyes, it is never beneficial to require this of them.

Applications and Modifications:
There are several modifications of this technique. The first modification would involve changing the nature of the treatment goal. In "The Wizard of Oz" Dorothy is missing home at the end of the movie. Children who have been adopted or moved to safe foster homes could use the technique to compare their old home to their new, safer home. These children could use the ruby slippers as a way of saying goodbye to the violent home. They could chant a mantra that gives closure to that chapter of their lives. For children awaiting adoption, the No Place Like Home technique could be used to help them flush out what their ideal home would look like. This will assist helping professionals in matching children to families.

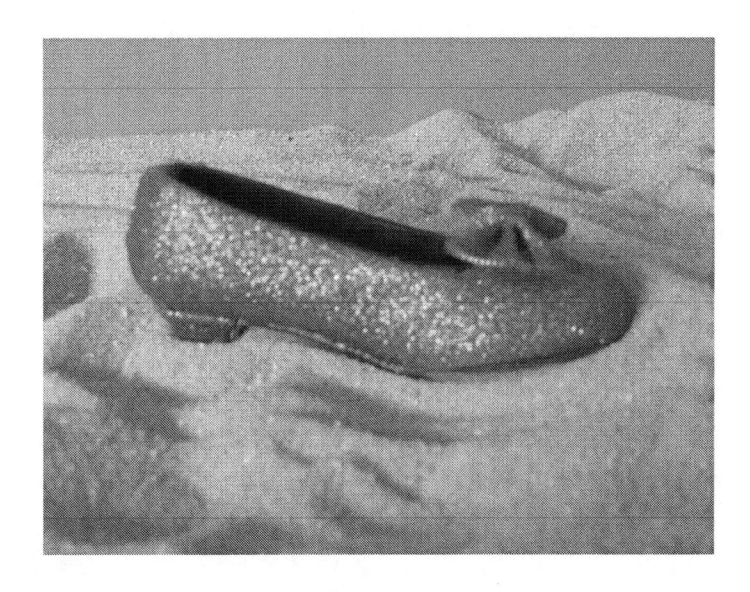

© Paris Goodyear-Brown, 2005. All Rights Reserved.

Learning to Bear It

Treatment Modality: Individual/Family
Population: Ages 6 to 12
Treatment Phase: Joining Phase

Treatment Goals:
1. To create a transitional object that can function as a connection between the safety of the play therapist and playroom to the rest of the child's environment
2. To increase the client's awareness of support systems
3. To mitigate against acting on suicidal thoughts by developing a no-harm contract
4. To help a client celebrate his achievements at termination

Props:
Autographable bear (These can be found at the Oriental Trading Company - see references)
Permanent markers

Procedure:
For traumatized children, the play therapist may be the only person with whom they truly feel safe. When this is the case, it benefits the child to maximize the influence of the

therapist by creating a transitional object. The little autographable bears used in this activity serve this purpose. The bears are made of foam or stuffing covered in clean white cotton or muslin. They were originally designed as a kind of yearbook for graduating children. Students have all their friends sign it as a way of remembering everyone who was in their class that year. These bears can serve as marvelous transitional objects in the therapy arena. To begin, present the bear to the child and talk about how we all need special friends some times. One of the best practices for suicidal clients involves designing a no-harm contract that serves as an official agreement between the therapist and client that the client will keep himself safe. After a written no-harm contract has been completed, the bear can serve as a place to write down the names and phone numbers of supportive people. The client is encouraged to call one of these people if he begins to think about hurting himself. The bear can also be used as the object on which various coping skills are recorded. If the client is dealing with anger management issues, each session could begin with the practice of a particular anger management skill. The session could end by writing the new skill on the bear. At the end of treatment, the client would have a nurturing reminder of the therapeutic process that also clearly delineates the anger management skills that are being generalized to other life arenas.

Processing Questions:

List the people that you can talk to when you start to think about hurting yourself.

What are there names? What are their phone numbers?

What are some new coping skills that you have learned during treatment? Write these on the bear.

What are some positive things that you have learned about yourself? Write these on the bear.

Homework Assignment:
Ask the client to put the bear in a prominent place at home. Ask the parent to read the statements/names/coping skills on the bear to the child each night before bed.

Special Considerations:
Young children may benefit from having pictures of coping skills drawn on the bear, as opposed to written statements. Young children are also likely to imbue the bear with life. The therapist can build on this developmental leaning by creating a voice for the bear and having the bear make positively affirming statements to the child. The bear could also serve as the guide in stress inoculation training or guided imagery and visualization activities as the therapist gives the bear a voice.

Applications and Modifications:
Another valuable use of the autographable bear is as an aid in the termination process. The therapist could choose to wait until the termination phase begins to introduce the bear. Explain that the bear will go home with the child and will help the child remember the time spent in the playroom, the gains made, etc. The client can write or draw pictures of favorite activities in the playroom and important therapeutic milestones. Finally, the therapist can write positive qualities that she sees in the client. The client can take the bear home and read the positive affirmations to himself whenever he wants to remember the therapist and the therapeutic experience.

© Paris Goodyear-Brown, 2005. All Rights Reserved.

© Paris Goodyear-Brown, 2005. All Rights Reserved.   37

Crowning Community

Treatment Modality: Individual/Group/Family
Population: Ages 4 to 18
Treatment Phase: Beginning/Working phase

Treatment Goals:
1. To help clients become aware of their social support network
2. To assist clients in combating the sense of isolation which often accompanies traumatic experiences
3. To help clients practice asking for help from social supports

Props:
Constuction paper or white paper
Paper doll template
Scissors
Masking tape/stapler
Glitter
Crayons/markers

Procedure:

Children who have been traumatized often feel isolated. They may believe that there is no one who will understand their experience and therefore they attempt to cope with their traumatic experiences alone. One of the strategies for reducing symptomatology in traumatized children is increasing the client's awareness and successful utilization of community supports. This activity is a fun way to help accomplish these goals. Begin by showing the child the paper doll template. Show the child how to fold a piece of paper into several layers so that once the folds of paper are cut out from the paper doll template, the result will be a paper doll chain. Two to three pieces of paper may need to be used, depending on how many support people the client lists. Each paper doll in the chain is labeled with the name of a support person. If the child has difficulty coming up with names of people who support her, the therapist must take an active role in pinpointing support systems for the client. As names are listed, the client is invited to clothe or decorate each of the paper dolls in the chain to help the doll resemble the person more closely. The child may add gray hair and glasses to one in order to represent her grandmother. She may add a girl scout uniform to represent her girl scout troop leader. Be sure to write the name of each supportive person on his or her corresponding paper doll. In fact, phone numbers can be added to the dolls as well. Then, if the client feels like talking to someone, she has a visual list of names and numbers to call. Help the client to exhaust her list of supports. The number of people available to help the child is often greater than the child believes. When the chain is complete, tape the first and last dolls to each other to create a crown or a necklace for the client.

Processing Questions:
Who are some people that you can talk to when you are sad or scared?
Who are some people that you can play with when you want to have fun?
Who can you snuggle with when you need a hug?
Who can answer important questions for you?
Who can you tell if something makes you uncomfortable?

Homework Assignment:
Have the client take home the paper doll chain and two or three additional paper doll cut outs. Encourage the client to keep thinking about supportive people during the week. As they go to school and to other activities, they may see or remember people that they could not remember during treatment. Using the take home dolls, the client can dress them up and add them to the crown or necklace.

Special Considerations:
Children who are struggling with shame about what happened to them may be reluctant to engage in this activity. Clients do not have to tell everyone what happened to them, but they must have a safe, supportive circle in which they can share. Explore the resistance expressed by clients who can't generate the names of many support people and be sure that the underlying issues of shame, mistrust and embarrassment are being dealt with concurrently in treatment.

Applications and Modifications:
This activity can be even more helpful if the parent or caregiver is present while the chain is being created. The parent can augment the list of support people and the parent is more likely to know phone numbers that can be added to the cut outs.

© Paris Goodyear-Brown, 2005. All Rights Reserved.

Personalized Pinwheels

Treatment Modality: Individual/Group/Family
Population: Ages 4 to 18
Treatment Phase: Initial/ Working Phase

Treatment Goals:
1. To educate the client about role of stress inoculation training in reducing trauma symptoms
2. To teach the client a deep breathing strategy
3. To help the client combat nocturnal anxiety

Props:
Paper
Pens
Pinwheels (different shapes and sizes)

© Paris Goodyear-Brown, 2005. All Rights Reserved.

Procedure:

Stress inoculation is important for traumatized children. One of the discrete skills that we want clients to acquire is the ability to regulate their breathing. When children begin to feel scared or to remember a past trauma, their breathing may become short and shallow. This increases feelings of panic and loss of control. Teaching a child how to take deep, slow, controlled breaths helps to counter the intense physical and emotional reactions that can accompany a response to trauma. Adults can generally be taught to control their breathing by counting methods. Children are more likely to master this skill if they are motivated by an external focal point.

Some play therapy techniques utilize bubbles as this point of focus, but in this activity pinwheels serve as the focusing point for the child. Begin by showing the child a variety of pinwheels. Ask the child to choose the smallest one, hold it close to his mouth and blow. The pinwheel should spin quite easily. Then ask the child to hold the same pinwheel as far away from his mouth as his arm will reach. Have the child try again to make it spin. The child will instinctively take a deeper, more focused breath and blow it out with more force. Ask the child about what he had to do differently to move the pinwheel that was farther away. Explain the relationship between anxiety (or "scary feelings about the bad thing that happened") and controlled breathing strategies. The child may explore various levels of breathing by using pinwheels of different shapes and sizes. The therapist can make the activity more challenging by holding the pinwheel and moving it, by degrees, farther and farther away from the child. Pinwheels can be purchased in bulk inexpensively through mail-order catalogs. Keep a bag of average sized pinwheels on hand and invite the client to choose one and personalize it. There are generally four flaps on a pinwheel. Therapist and client can generate four self-soothing statements that the client can say to himself, write them on small slips of paper and glue them on the inside of each flap of the pinwheel. This will encourage cognitive work while the kinesthetic activity (deep breathing) is happening.

Processing Questions:
How does it feel when you take in short quick breaths?
How does it feel when you take a deep breath in and blow it out slowly?
What do you have to do to blow the pinwheel as it gets farther from you?
What are some thoughts you can tell yourself when you need to calm down?
What are some times when taking a deep breath might help you calm down?

Homework Assignment:
Invite the caregiver into the room. Have the client show the caregiver how he can blow the pinwheel while the therapist moves it farther and farther away. Ask the client to share his self-soothing statements with the caregiver. Invite the child and caregiver to practice blowing the pinwheel before bed every night. The child can read one of his self-soothing statements off the pinwheel and then blow it. The parent can hold the pinwheel at various degrees of distance and encourage the child to take deep, controlled breaths.

Special Considerations:
Young children will not be able to read the words written on the pinwheels. Pictures attached to the pinwheel points might be more helpful. Another alternative would be to teach the parent the soothing statements and have the parent say them and the child repeat them each night as the activity is practiced.

© Paris Goodyear-Brown, 2005. All Rights Reserved.

Applications and Modifications:

Many clients have particular difficulty going to sleep at night. If their abuse happened during the night, they may become more and more anxious as bedtime approaches. For these clients, a glow-in-the-dark pinwheel can be very effective. Clients are still taught self-soothing statements to say to themselves while blowing the pinwheel. However, these pinwheels can be held to the light before the light is turned off for the night and they will hold the glow. The child then has a "triple whammy" of relaxation: the focal point of light in the darkened room, the object's association with the therapist and the safety of the playroom, and the kinesthetic release of tension that comes from taking the deep breaths while lying in bed. This activity is also lots of fun in a group setting. Larger pinwheels, including the kind that are often put in gardens and blown by the wind, can be used. All group members put their heads together and use their combined breath to try and blow these larger pinwheels.

Empowerment Exercises for Traumatized Clients

Megaphones to Make a Point

Treatment Modality: Individual/Group/Family
Population: Ages 5 to adult
Treatment Phase: Working phase

Treatment Goals:

1. To help clients express internal states verbally
2. To empower clients to make their needs clear
3. To amplify the abuse survivor's voice while confronting the perpetrator
4. To practice maintaining appropriate verbal boundaries in conversation

Props:
Plastic play megaphone (these can sometimes be found at Dollar Stores or novelty shops)
Large construction paper
Tape
Markers, paint, etc.

© Paris Goodyear-Brown, 2005. All Rights Reserved.

Procedure:

This intervention has many adaptations and can be especially useful for survivors of abuse. Many of the children who are seen in treatment have lost their voice. Indeed, some of our clients have never had a chance to use their voices. The megaphone functions as both a symbol of power and a mechanism for amplifying the voices of our clients. Begin by introducing the child to the megaphone. Ask the child if she have ever seen a megaphone used. The child may say that she has seen it on T.V.; perhaps a coach used one on the ball field to communicate with players; perhaps the director of the school play used one to call directions to actors on stage. Once the child has a context for the megaphone's use, the therapist introduces the idea of using the megaphone in the playroom to say some things that need saying. It is often easier for children to engage in an activity when the therapist models how to do it. In this case, the therapist would give an example of a time in her life when someone said something to hurt her feelings. The therapist might say "When I was little, there was this bully in school and he took my lunch one day. I was too afraid to say anything to him at the time, but I wish I'd had one of these. If I could use this megaphone and tell him something, I would say, 'Give me back my lunch right now!'" The therapist says the empowering phrase aloud one time, then uses the megaphone to say it again. Tell the client that practicing the things one wants to say with the megaphone in the playroom makes it easier to say the things that need saying in other places.

Ask the child if there has been a time when someone hurt her feelings or took something from her. Another approach would be to ask her to think of a time when she didn't feel heard. The most reserved children may have difficulty thinking of what they want to say and need to be jumpstarted with a good story - perhaps a traditional fairy tale. Ask the child to take the perspective of the protagonist. What would the princess want to say to the evil witch? Once the child gets

© Paris Goodyear-Brown, 2005. All Rights Reserved.

used to making forceful verbalizations, the activity can be brought back to the child's own experiences.

The child can make her own megaphone out of construction paper. It can be personalized with words and drawings that are meaningful to the child. The drawings may be depictions of the child as strong and courageous. The words may include some of the messages the child wants to amplify to a perpetrator (like "It's not my fault" or "You're a liar") or even the resolutions to stressful situations that may accompany the child's new ability to be heard.

Processing Questions:
What was it like to hear your voice in the megaphone?
What was the first statement that you wanted others to hear louder?
Who would you like to use this newer, clearer voice with?
How can you be heard as clearly as you are with the megaphone without having to be so loud?

Homework Assignment:
Choose one of the statements that you spoke into the megaphone and practice saying it in context. (An example: When your brother teases you, say "I don't like it. Stop or I won't play with you anymore." Have the client practice saying it forcefully, but without yelling. Report back to the therapist next session.

Special Considerations:
Some children have been so abused and beaten down that this kind of activity may be impossible for them early on in treatment. The therapist will need to spend lots of time helping the client feel safe and secure in the playroom before the megaphone is introduced. Moreover, the client may need several more modeling sessions from the therapist before she is willing to try it herself.

© Paris Goodyear-Brown, 2005. All Rights Reserved.

Applications and Modifications:

Many victims of abuse are terrified of confronting their perpetrators even in the safety of the playroom. Yet some of the most important work that clients do will be to pit their voices against the lies of their perpetrators. One way to make the exercise more powerful and more playful is to have the child choose a puppet to represent the perpetrator. The puppet must obey all the instructions of the child. The child commands through the megaphone and the puppet must comply. Alternatively, the puppet could make statements like the lies that the child has been fed by the perpetrator, only this time the child overpowers the lying voice with truth spoken through the megaphone.

In family therapy, the megaphone can function as a reminder of who has the floor to talk. Also, each family member gets a turn with the megaphone and actually orchestrates or directs the other family members in a "play" that depicts the way that family member would like to see the family interact.

Blow the Whistle on 'Em

Treatment Modality: Individual/Group/Family
Population: Ages 5 to 12
Treatment Phase: Working phase

Treatment Goals:
1. To educate the client about the concept of verbal boundaries
2. To help the client become aware of inappropriate verbalizations
3. To empower clients to set verbal boundaries
4. To practice maintaining appropriate verbal boundaries in conversation

Props:
Flat whistle
Traditional whistle
Bicycle horn (optional)

Procedure:
This technique was designed in response to the many children who have poor verbal boundaries. Children who are unable to discern the difference between appropriate and inappropriate

conversation can become the targets of sexual perpetrators and school yard bullies alike. There are several programs available to teach the difference between good touches and bad touches, but the line between appropriate and inappropriate verbalizations is much more confusing and less clearly articulated to children. An example might help. A nine year old girl was sexually molested for one year by an extended family member. When this client began to process her abusive experiences, it became clear that the perpetrator crossed many verbal boundaries before he began crossing physical boundaries. This grooming tactic is common. I had the client repeat the verbalizations that the perpetrator made to her. I then gave the client a whistle and we role played similar conversations. Her job was to "blow the whistle" on "the perpetrator" any time that she began to feel uncomfortable. The therapist must immediately stop talking when the child blows the whistle. This gives the child a tremendous sense of control which the therapist can augment by being dramatic about the cut off.

In this activity, the therapist can make the verbalizations (as long as the client is comfortable with the pretend nature of the activity). A puppet or other playroom prop can also be used as the perpetrator and the verbalizations can come from this source. The client will usually giggle the first few times that she blows the whistle on you. It can be argued that the giggling is a measure of the child's anxiety as she confronts - in role play - the inappropriate speech of the perpetrator. The laughter may also be an indicator of the empowerment that the child feels by being able to stop the abusive words with a breath.

It is fun to play around with which particular kind of noisemaker chosen to stop the inappropriate words. Various novelty companies sell flat whistles as well as traditional whistles. I even found a bicycle horn shaped like an alligator that makes a very loud honking sound when squeezed. Boys may be especially drawn to train whistles. The child could even try yelling "stop" or something equally forceful. The client will practice this activity over and over again. While he is feeling powerful at being able to finally stop the flow of words that has made him so uncomfortable in the past, he is also practicing setting new verbal boundaries in a kinesthetic way. Once this whistle blowing technique has been practiced several times, explain to the client that he may not always have a whistle handy when he would like to use one and that his own words can function as the whistle. Then teach the client two or three verbalizations to practice. These might include, "I don't like talking about that", "This conversation is making me uncomfortable", or even "Stop right now or I'll tell my mom".

Processing Questions:
What are some words that you like hearing?
What are some words or questions that make you uncomfortable?
How can you recognize that the words someone is saying are bothering you?
What can you do to let someone know that you don't like what they have said?

Homework Assignment:
Once the child has practiced blowing the whistle in the playroom, encourage them to listen out for inappropriate verbalizations in their environment (school, home, etc.). Ask them to bring in a list of two or three inappropriate statements or words they've heard during the previous week to the next session. An alternative assignment would be to have them practice a particular whistle blowing phrase like, "That makes me uncomfortable" at least twice in the next week.

Special Considerations:
Children who have been sexually abused may have difficulty even identifying the statements that their perpetrators made while being abusive. The clinician then has to take an active role in

educating the client about appropriate and inappropriate verbalizations in the same way that clinicians educate about good and bad touch. This technique should not be used during an ongoing investigation of abuse as the "education" may be seen as contamination. Also, if the clinician repeats the words of the perpetrator it must be in a way that is far removed from reality and would not confuse the client about the actual boundaries between the therapist and the client. If the client at any point becomes anxious or confused, the intervention should be terminated.

Applications and Modifications:

This technique, while designed for children who have already been sexually compromised, could easily become an extension of a preventative personal safety curriculum for all children. This tool is equally valuable for helping children with externalizing disorders to assess their own inappropriate verbalizations. Often we see children who bully and are verbally abusive to other children, or who use inappropriate language with others. This game can be used to help these clients confront their own abusive behavior.

© Paris Goodyear-Brown, 2005. All Rights Reserved.

Door Hangers

Treatment Modality: Individual/Group/Family
Population: Ages 3 to 18
Treatment Phase: Working phase

Treatment Goals:
1. To educate the client about the concept of physical boundaries
2. To help the client become aware of dysfunctional boundaries within the family
3. To help the client delineate clear boundaries with family members
4. To help family members practice keeping those boundaries

Props:
Foam door hangers
Foam shapes and letters
(felt or construction paper might be a cheap alternative)
Glue

Procedure:
This technique is based on the tenants of family systems theory and attempts to impact the boundary problems common in families who come to treatment. Some families tend towards

disengagement. This may be evidenced by family members having a "closed door policy". Each family member lives fairly separate lives. They come home, go up to their own rooms, lock their doors and talk on the phone, play video games, watch T.V., etc. Other families tend towards enmeshment. The doors are never closed in these families. In fact, they may function as if doors do not exist. Children sleep in mom and dad's bed every night, mom and dad never have a date night away from the kids, and the kids get no privacy. Many of these dynamics in dysfunctional families are not readily assessed during the initial interview. Door hangers help to broach this subject.

Begin by asking the child/parent if he has a door hanger. If he does not, introduce the idea of making one during the session. Generally, showing the child the pre-cut foam door hanger will generate interest in the activity. Discuss the various uses of door hangers with the client. Give examples. Hotel door hangers can say anything from, "Do not disturb!" to "change the linens, please" to a request to have breakfast sent to your room. Ask the child what sorts of messages he would want to have on his door. Have the child decorate both sides of the door hanger. Children are likely to want to make incendiary messages like "Keep Out!!" This is a valid message for children who have been given no privacy and no sense of respect. Try to help the child state the need for privacy politely. Examples include: "Taking alone time now", or "Having private time", or "Please knock before entering." The other side of the door hanger can be used to request a particular kind of interaction from other family members. Examples include: "Come in and hang", "Available for conversation", or "Need some TLC". Once the door hanger is complete, it's use and meaning must be processed with the whole family. Encourage all family members to honor the new boundaries. The child may need limits set on how frequently and for what duration the hanger can be used. Children who have not had clearly delineated boundaries up to this point may want to have the "Keep Out" side up all the time. Help the child to create a balanced use of the sign as both limit and invitation.

© Paris Goodyear-Brown, 2005. All Rights Reserved.

Processing Questions:
Does your door remain open or closed most of the time?
If a family member wants something from you, how do they get it?
What kind of communication would you like to increase in your family?
What communications would you like to decrease in your family?
How would it feel if your family members honored the signals on your door hanger?
How could you show them that you appreciate their new behavior?

Homework Assignment:
Help the family choose a time to do a "test run" with the sign. This should be set up as an at-home role play. The child puts the sign on the door (at a time that the parents are expecting - either after school, before bed, etc.) and family members get an opportunity to "practice" honoring the signs. Part of the homework assignment is that the child rewards the parents in some obvious way for honoring the signs.

Special Considerations:
Children who already have rigid boundaries would not benefit from this technique. While adolescents will appreciate the systemic issues, the technique will function as a behavioral intervention with younger children. Children will be trained to respect the boundaries of, for example, the parents' bedroom. At the same time the parents are learning that children should receive privacy and respect.

Applications and Modifications:
This technique was originally intended for use in family treatment. It could, however, be modified to work well with groups of children. All of the supplies for making the door hangers would be placed in the middle of the table. The

therapist invites conversation about boundaries (this may require some psycho-education that defines the concept of "boundaries"). Each child in the group makes his own door hanger. Then each child shares his creation with the group. One of the benefits of using this technique with a group is that each child is exposed to the boundaries of other children. Through this processing session, children learn that boundaries can vary from person to person and from relationship to relationship. This is an important awareness in the evolution of healthy social interaction.

© Paris Goodyear-Brown, 2005. All Rights Reserved.

Keep Your Hands Off Me

Treatment Modality: Individual/Group/Family
Population: Ages 7 to 18
Treatment Phase: Working phase

Treatment Goals:
1. To help the client organize a verbal response to the perpetrator's actions
2. To empower the client to verbally confront the perpetrator in play
3. To assist clients in combating the lies of the perpetrator
4. To connect verbalizations with kinesthetic activity for a deeper experience of catharsis

Props:
A jump rope

Procedure:
Children who have been abused are often terrified of their perpetrators. This terror serves to inhibit the expression of any other emotion in treatment. Often, children will come to treatment and talk about the facts of the traumas they have

experienced. The children will discuss the events in a monotone voice and with blunted affect. There is no distinction made between everyday events and traumatic events because in the mind of the child, traumatic events have become the norm. In order to survive the abusive situation, the child will keep a tight reign on all emotions. This eventually leads to a disconnect between the client's mind and body. When a child comes to treatment with this kind of a disconnect, she is unable to touch the anger that she may feel towards the perpetrator. Many times, this anger has been turned inward and the client is engaging in self-injurious behaviors. This technique is intended to help the client externalize some of her anger towards the perpetrator while re-establishing a connection between her mind and body. The original technique was generated during a session with a 9 year old girl who had been sexually molested by an extended family member. When the little girl came to treatment, she was able to tell me, in hushed tones, what her perpetrator had done to her. This little girl came from a fairly high functioning family and had been raised to be well mannered and polite. All the details of her abuse were thus presented in a polite, but emotionally disengaged manner. After the child had finished going through the laundry list of what had happened to her, I asked, "While he was doing those things, what would you have liked to say to him." The little girl thought for a moment, smiled shyly, and then said very politely, "Please stop doing that." I smiled back at her and said, "Well, you know what I want to say to him..." Then I picked up a jump rope and jumped it while saying loudly, "KEEP YOUR HANDS OFF ME!" I watched her affect closely to see if I was on the right track. The little girl grinned widely and said, "Let me try!" She took the jump rope and began jumping. She repeated the phrase, "Keep your hands off me," stating one word with each jump. Her voice started off softly and rose with each repetition of the phrase. Afterwards, the client reported feeling relieved and left the session lighter than when she had arrived.

© Paris Goodyear-Brown, 2005. All Rights Reserved.

The use of kinesthetic activity combined with verbalization in the outward channeling of anger is a powerful combination. Requiring the child to verbalize something in relation to her perpetrator engages her cognitive faculties while the full body movement necessitated by jumping rope engages her body. The combination allows for the mind and body to re-connect to each other and for anger catharsis to occur. The client should feel relieved afterward. In fact, the client may often breathe a deep sigh after engaging in this activity. Girls, particularly, have been socialized to hold anger inside. It is impossible to jump rope and verbalize at the same time without taking deep breaths. Deep breathing and verbalization combined with the intense kinesthetic movement encourages a more dramatic expulsion of feeling.

Processing Questions:
If you could say anything to your perpetrator without fear of being hurt again, what would you want to say?
What did you feel in your body when you were jumping rope?
What was it like to say those words while jumping rope?
How do you feel now that you've done it?

Homework Assignment:
Ask the parent to provide a jump rope for the child at home (these can be found very cheaply at discount stores). Have the parent coach the child through this same activity two to three times during the following week. Check in with the parent about an increase or decrease in symptomatology at the end of this time.

Special Considerations:
The therapist will need to carefully assess the client's gross motor development before attempting this activity. Since this activity is aimed at integrating the mind and the body in order to provide an anger catharsis experience, it could be

detrimental to attempt this with a client who is not competent at jumping rope. Secondly, the emotional expression that often results from this exercise can be quite powerful. Clinicians will want to make sure that the trust relationship between client and therapist is strong, and that the client's personality structure can handle this strong an expression of anger. Lastly, this technique is contraindicated for children who already have impulse control issues related to violent anger ventilation.

Applications and Modifications:

This technique has been modified to do with a whole group at once. This can be particularly empowering when done with a group of sexual abuse or domestic violence survivors. In this case, the therapist would give the same prompt to all participants, asking them to generate a statement that they would like to make to their perpetrator. In a large space, each client would be given a jump rope. On the count of three all participants would begin to jump and verbalize together (this minimizes the sort of embarrassment that comes from any one client being singled out). After the group has done it together, the therapist may ask if any member would like to repeat the exercise in front of the whole group. Clients will often find that their peers are making similar statements to theirs. More importantly, they may sense the same intensity of affect being released by their peers, thereby normalizing the intensity of their own anger towards the perpetrator.

Puppet on a String

Treatment Modality: Individual/Family
Population: Ages 5 to 18
Treatment Phase: Working phase

Treatment Goals:
1. To help clients articulate the coercive behaviors of their perpetrators
2. To empower clients to stop blaming themselves for the abuse
3. To allow clients to practice resisting the manipulations of potential perpetrators
4. To give the clients a metaphoric experience of being free from the perpetrator's control

Props:
A range of marionettes
Styrofoam balls
Scarves
String
Sticks

© Paris Goodyear-Brown, 2005. All Rights Reserved.

Procedure:

This technique grew out of the confusion faced by many child survivors of abuse. Abused children have been made to say and do things that they would not naturally have done. However, once an abused child has done the bidding of the perpetrator, the child often begins to believe that they chose the behavior. Children become confused about whether or not they wanted or deserved the abuse. Children who have been forced to lie to other important people in their lives may own a significant amount of guilt related to the lies.

In this activity, the child begins to understand that she was manipulated by her perpetrator. A marionette or "puppet on a string" serves as the metaphor through which the client can explore the ways in which she was controlled and manipulated by her abuser. Begin by introducing a couple of marionettes to the client. The client may choose one to represent herself, or she may create one out of the materials listed above. Have the client list two or three of the behaviors that she engaged in during the abusive experience. Write these down. Once the list has been created, take each behavior in turn and help the client remember where the action originated. For example, the client may feel guilty for sitting on the perpetrator's lap. Usually, if the memory is reconstructed, it becomes apparent that the perpetrator first asked, coerced or commanded the client to sit on his lap. Have the client take on the voice of the perpetrator while manipulating the marionette into doing the required behavior. In the example above, the client would take the sticks of the marionette and say, "Come sit on my lap and I'll read you a story," while she makes the marionette sit in his lap. If the client cannot remember a direct statement or action made by the abuser, reframe the guilt-inducing behavior in terms of survival. Survivors of abuse have often engaged in behavior without the direct verbal command of a perpetrator in order to avoid retribution or make the horror of the situation more manageable. All of these behaviors are still grounded in the control the child feels emanating from the perpetrator. After the manipulations have been processed, the real fun begins. The client gets to generate a response to the perpetrator that takes back some control. She might say, "I told someone anyway." As she says each of these empowering statements she cuts one of the strings, thereby getting a kinesthetic and visual experience of being freed from the perpetrator's manipulations.

Processing Questions:
What did the person who hurt you make you do?
Which parts of what happened were the most yucky for you?
Who made you do these things?
How did you get out of the situation?
What are some things you did or said that helped you get free?

Homework Assignment:
Have the client write down the words and behaviors that accompany the cutting of the strings. Have her read over these at least once a day between sessions to remind herself that she exerted some power to get out of the traumatic situation.

Special Considerations:
It should be clear from the description of this exercise that this activity is for use with clients who have disclosed their abuse and are safe. A client must be out from underneath the threat of the perpetrator in order to engage in this kind of processing. The activity then becomes, in part, a celebration of the resiliencies within the child that helped her get free from the abuse. Younger children will need lots of help from the therapist in designing their own marionettes, but the investment that these clients will then have in the activity is worth the energy expended on the front end.

© Paris Goodyear-Brown, 2005. All Rights Reserved.

Applications and Modifications:

One modification of this technique shifts the focus to the child's fantasies regarding her disposition of the perpetrator. The child can design a marionette to represent the perpetrator and then can control his strings. This activity puts the survivor "in charge" of the perpetrator in an experiential way. The client may walk the perpetrator over to the jail, make him sit in a corner, stand on his head or apologize for his actions twenty times in a row. The child gets to engage in wish fulfillment in a kinesthetic way.

Sensory Processing Exercises for Trauma Survivors

See No Evil, Hear No Evil...

Treatment Modality: Individual/Family
Population: 4 and up
Treatment Phase: Working phase

Treatment Goals:
1. To help the child process sensory information from trauma
2. To help the child externalize the sensory information
3. To help the child integrate sensory memories from trauma into the narrative of what happened

Props:
Sand tray
Three monkeys (preferably the ones with hands covering eyes, ears, and mouth)
Strips of paper
Markers

Procedure:
This technique is meant to help a child process sensory information related to a trauma she has experienced. As we delve into a series of techniques that will help children process this kind of information, I want to be clear that not all children

© Paris Goodyear-Brown, 2005. All Rights Reserved.

need to reprocess the events of their trauma. Indeed, many children who have been traumatized find ways to cope with the trauma and are able to function at high levels in all arenas of life. It is primarily when children are stuck in their traumas that re-processing of this nature is helpful. "Stuckness" is often present when a child is continuing to struggle with intrusive symptoms such as nightmares or flashbacks, continuous disregulation or hyperarousal, or extreme avoidance of people, places or things that interferes with normal functioning. When these symptoms are present, strategies that encourage the brain to integrate somatosensory memories with linear narrative information can be helpful.

Begin by placing three monkeys equal distances apart in the sandtray. Monkey figurines that represent the old "hear no evil, see no evil, speak no evil" would be perfect, but three non-descript monkeys would also work. Sing the "Hear no evil" song for the child. Then give the child paper and a marker and ask the child to draw a picture of one thing she wished she hadn't heard during the trauma. It might be the sound of someone screaming or the sound of tires screeching. The child is invited to fold up the picture and tuck it in the sand under the monkey. Then ask the child to draw a picture about one thing that she didn't want to see and have her put it under the second monkey. Lastly, ask the child about one thing she wished she hadn't had to say. This question often produces the most interesting responses. One client's response was "I wish I hadn't had to ask my mom so many times to play with me." This client's mother was drug addicted and, while taking care of his basic needs, often neglected to nurture him. Having the children place the pictures or statements underneath the sand aids in breaking down resistance to the re-processing of these memories. Children often feel pressured to give the right kind of verbal answer when asked questions by adults. In this scenario, the child will not be directly confronted. The therapist asks the question, the client draws a picture or writes a statement and buries it in the sand and the therapist looks at it later.

© Paris Goodyear-Brown, 2005. All Rights Reserved.

Processing Questions:
How easy or difficult was it to remember one thing you heard? Saw? Said?
How did it feel to write it down and put it in the sand?
If you could go back and say one thing that you didn't say then, what would it be?

Homework Assignment:
Explain to the client that beginning to focus on sensory memories related to the trauma may spark further memories that had previously been suppressed. Help the client choose a method for recording any other somatosensory memories that come up during the week and a safe place for storing them. Invite the client to bring any newly uncovered details to the next session.

Special Considerations:
Any work that involves taking a child back through somatosensory details of a trauma must be carefully timed. The child must have a strong working relationship with the therapist and trust the therapist to buffer the client from being re-traumatized while revisiting some of the specific impressions caused by the original trauma. Co-regulation of affect and helping the client to remain grounded in the here-and-now are important functions of the therapist during this activity.

Applications and Modifications:
Each client's trauma is unique and the memories stored at the sensory level will be idiosyncratic. Due to the sensitive and sometimes gruesome nature of the memories, this technique would be contraindicated for use in a group setting. First of all, the level of trust that is needed to engage in this kind of

work would probably not *be* present in adequate amounts in relation to each group member. Secondly, as one person is drawing or writing their memory, another group member might *see* or hear it. If this detail is more gruesome than anything experienced in his or her own trauma, this child might *be* secondarily traumatized *by* the telling. This technique could *be* done in a family setting if the therapist has already worked to make sure that family members are strong supports for each other and will *be* able to appropriately contain each other's perceptions of the event.

Monster Ears

Treatment Modality: Individual/Family
Population: Ages 3 to 18
Treatment Phase: Working phase

Treatment Goals:
1. To help the client become aware of auditory memories that may be impacting the client's response to a traumatic event
2. To help the client verbally process the auditory memory
3. To confront the client's potentially inaccurate linguistic narrative
4. To reconstruct an accurate narrative of the traumatic event that integrates the auditory information

Props:
Monster Ears (see picture)
Potential noise making devices

Procedure:
This technique was created in response to the large number of clients seen in treatment who have witnessed traumatic events.

Sometimes this witnessing has been primarily auditory. In domestic violence situations, the child is often hiding under a table or behind a piece of furniture while the adults are yelling at each other. Children are often sent to their rooms while the parents have a verbal or physical altercation. The adults believe that the client is protected from absorbing the violence because they are not witnessing it with their eyes. These children often engage in heightened auditory encoding of the violence. They automatically encode auditory memories of the traumatic event, (i.e. the sound of glass breaking, raised voices, doors slamming, etc.). Children then construct visual memories based on this auditory encoding, filling in the gaps with their imagination. Auditory input connected to abusive situations can then become trauma triggers for these children, so that a teacher who raises her voice in frustration with a client may inadvertently trigger a trauma response (such as freezing or sudden disregulation of affect or behavior) in the child. When recall of traumatic events interferes with the normal functioning of a child, it can be helpful to reprocess the auditory data associated with the trauma. Monster ears are enlarged rubber ears that can be purchased from a novelty store or costume shop. They fit right over a child's own ears and counter the intensity of the work with their silliness.

Begin by explaining the role of auditory memory to the child. You might say, "When mommies and daddies fight, kids hear a lot of scary things. Some children hear things breaking, others remember ugly words that their parents said to each other, etc. It can be scary to remember these sounds and words, but sometimes remembering them with a caring adult can make them less scary." Then invite the child to put on the monster ears. (You may need to put one on your own ear to show the child how they work-and to give permission for the silliness.) Explain that the monster ears allow the child to remember in greater detail the sounds that went on during the trauma. It may be easier for the child to isolate the auditory input if he closes his eyes, but this should be made as a suggestion that the child can accept or reject. After the child

© Paris Goodyear-Brown, 2005. All Rights Reserved.

verbalizes the sounds, you may invite the child to find a way to reproduce the sound in the playroom. She can smack the table to make a slapping or thumping sound, use a puppet with a funny voice to recreate the scary words that were spoken, etc. It could be useful to have a sealed container with some broken glass as one of the noise makers. When the child has recreated the sound, ask her what she believes was happening while those sounds were being made. Oftentimes children will fill in visual images based on auditory stimuli. These images may be worse than the truth of what actually happened. For example, a child might remember hearing shattering glass and fill in a visual image of the father throwing a pickle jar at the mother and cutting her face with it. The actual truth might be that the father threw the pickle jar at the wall in his frustration. If the truth (based on your assessment with the caregiver(s)) is less scary than the narrative the child has constructed, the caregiver can be invited to come in and help the client reconstruct what actually happened. If a caregiver is unavailable, the therapist can aid in the reconstruction.

Processing Questions:
What is the sound that you remember the most from that scary time?
What other noises, words, etc. do you remember hearing while the scary thing was happening? (You want to exhaust the list of auditory memories associated with this particular trauma.)
Based on these noises, what do you believe happened?
Who can we talk to in order to find out what really happened?

Homework Assignment:
Explain to the child that focusing on auditory memories in session may make them more aware of the noises around them for awhile. Ask the child to find one song, piece of music or soothing sound that they can listen to as needed. Ask the child to listen to this soothing sound three times a day everyday until

their next session. When scary images related to the trauma come up, ask the child to again listen to the soothing sound, or have a caregiver sing the song.

Special Considerations:
This technique, like any of the reprocessing strategies listed in this text, requires a high degree of trust and rapport between the client and the therapist. Therefore this technique is not appropriate for use during the beginning phase of treatment. In fact, the best practice is to have self-soothing strategies specifically related to the auditory sense in place before this exercise is attempted. Also, it is important to have practiced ways to keep the client grounded in the "here-and-now" before taking them back into traumatic material from earlier in life.

Applications and Modifications:
Due to the potentially intense nature of this intervention, it is not appropriate for use in a group setting. However, a family could engage in this activity together. It would be important to set ground rules for family members to remain quiet and listen while another member processes their trauma memory through the auditory sense. After all are finished, they may compare their auditory memories and engage in reconstructing a coherent and accurate narrative of the traumatic event together.

Putting the Pieces Together Again

Treatment Modality: Individual/Family
Population: Ages 3 to 18
Treatment Phase: Working phase

Treatment Goals:
1. To aid the "stuck" client in identifying somatosensory memories related to a specific trauma
2. To help the client verbalize specific somatosensory memories
3. To assist the client in integrating these somatosensory memories into the linguistic narrative of the event

Props:
Wooden puzzles of faces (with removable eyes, ears, etc.)
Construction paper
Markers
Scissors
Tape
Brown paper bag

Procedure:
This technique was designed as another tool in aiding children to integrate their somatosensory memories into their linguistic

accounts of the trauma in order to create a coherent narrative. Begin by explaining to the child that each of our senses has a different function. Ask the child to describe what a nose does, what a mouth does, what eyes do, etc. The child will likely reply that the nose smells things, the mouth talks and tastes, the eyes see, etc. Explain that when a really bad or scary thing happens, these "sensing parts" of our body become even stronger and work even better than normal. You can give an example of a child who is in a car accident. She may remember the smell of the burning rubber or the sound of the crashing metal much more sharply than she remembers the sounds of bugs in her backyard. If you are dealing with a child who has had repeated traumatic experiences, you may encourage the child to choose one at a time for processing. If the child has experienced sexual abuse by the same person in the same setting (ie. the bed in the middle of the night), the child may have assimilated a lot of similar sounds, smells, etc. into impressions that characterized the longer-term abuse experience. If this is the case, the child may wish to talk about the somatosensory experiences related to the abuse as a whole instead of working through specific instances of the abuse.

Show the wooden puzzle to the child (these puzzles can be purchased through Constructive Playthings ™. Have the child dump out the eyes, ears, nose, etc. into a brown paper bag. The child is then invited to reach into the brown paper bag and choose a puzzle piece. Ask the child to feel the edges of the puzzle piece while her hand is still inside the bag and guess which part of the face it is. This part of the activity is aimed at helping the client focus more on physical sensations. She is using her tactile sensory knowledge to explore the puzzle piece without the use of her eyes. Once the child has withdrawn the puzzle piece from the bag, she tells one sensory memory connected to the trauma that is represented by the puzzle piece. If the client has chosen an ear then she shares one thing she heard while the abuse was happening. If she chose the nose, she will describe one thing she smelled during the

© Paris Goodyear-Brown, 2005. All Rights Reserved.

traumatic event. After the client has put all the pieces back into the puzzle, have the child compare her impressions of the face "with all the pieces missing" to the face "put back together again". The compartmentalization and dissociative nature of the empty face can be contrasted with the wholly integrated face.

Processing Questions:
How does this face look/feel with all the sensing parts missing? How does it look/feel when it is put back together again? What is one thing you smelled during the bad thing that happened? One thing you heard? Saw? Tasted? Felt?

Homework Assignment:
Inform the child that playing this puzzle game may have sent a message to the child's senses that it is now safe to remember other sensory information related to the bad thing that happened. Let the child know that she may remember other smells, sounds, sights, etc. during the next week. Help the child decide how this will be handled. Will they write them down in a journal or draw pictures? Have them choose a safe, available adult who they can talk to if memories come up between visits. Also, have the child practice her soothing sensory strategies every day (see below for details).

Special Considerations:
The integration of somatosensory memories into the factual account of a trauma narrative, while sometimes necessary, may be extremely uncomfortable for the child. Therefore, this work is only to be undertaken after the child has developed a set of soothing sensory strategies. The therapist needs to have completed the work of helping the client identify soothing sensory stimuli. Furthermore, the therapist needs to have helped the client practice envisioning these sensory stimuli when needed. The child should be able to readily imagine soothing

smells, sounds, words, visual images and physical sensations *before* this intervention is attempted.

Applications and Modifications:

This strategy is one of many listed in this section that target the intimate work of re-processing or integrating aspects of a traumatic event that continue to be problematic for the client. Therefore, this technique is not conducive to a group format. This exercise may be completed in a family session, especially if a parent or caregiver is an important attachment figure and can act as a second container or witness for the sensory content of the trauma. The decision about whether or not to include a caregiver in this session must be made carefully, as some caregivers have been so traumatized themselves that they are unable or unwilling to accept a containment role for the child.

One modification of this technique is to have the client draw a large self-portrait of her head. The child then cuts the eyes, ears, etc. out of the portrait. The idea of the game remains the same, only the child can write or draw the sensory memory on the back of each cut out part. The client tapes the parts back together as the game is played.

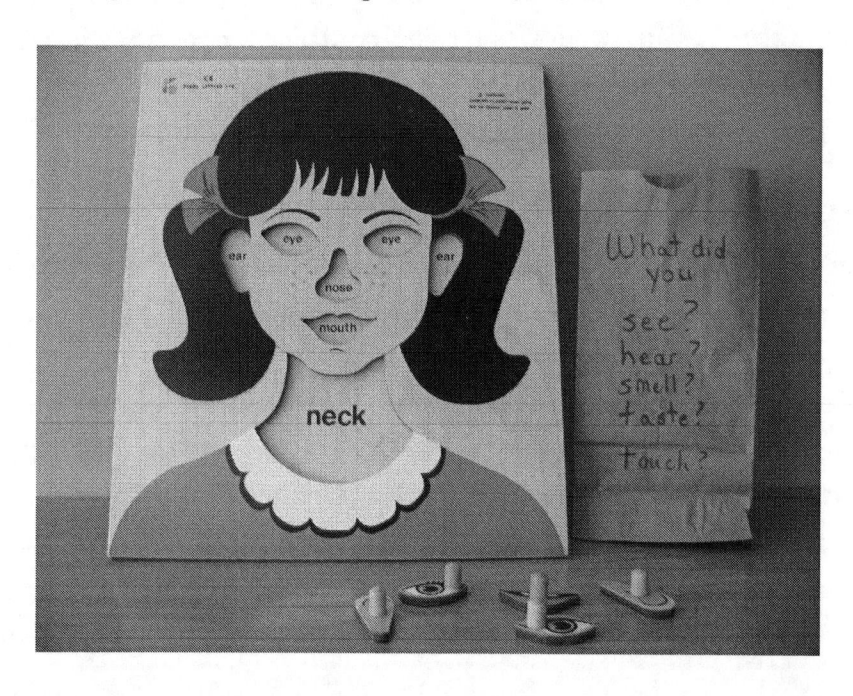

© Paris Goodyear-Brown, 2005. All Rights Reserved.

Pieces and Parts

Treatment Modality: Individual/Family
Population: Ages 3 to 15
Treatment Phase: Working phase

Treatment Goals:
1. To assist the traumatized client in processing information related to the perpetrator
2. To enable to client to engage in containment of the perpetrator symbol
3. To encourage the client to process the impact of the trauma on their sense of self

Props:
Puppet pieces (a set can be purchased that includes two blank hand puppets and many Velcro parts including assorted eyes, ears, noses, mouths, hands, feet, hair and other accessories)

© Paris Goodyear-Brown, 2005. All Rights Reserved.

Procedure:

Children who have been traumatized have lost a sense of their own power and their ability to control the environment. In the playroom, children can regain a sense of control by being allowed to deal with the symbols of their perpetrators in whatever ways they choose. Most children, once they have chosen or created a perpetrator symbol find a way to contain it (i.e. they put the symbol in jail, tie it up or otherwise manipulate it). In this way they strip the perpetrator of power and control and experience a sense of empowerment themselves. This activity is one way of giving the client permission to approach the perpetrator symbolically while encouraging empowerment. Begin by putting all the puppet parts in the middle of the table or floor. Explain to the child that all kinds of characters can be created from these puppets. Invite the child to create a puppet that represents the "person who hurt him". Give permission for this puppet to look any way the child chooses (it does not have to be physically accurate). Children will often add parts that are symbolic of the abuse or aspects of the abuse. The picture below is an example of this phenomenon. This client gave the perpetrator a "tail" because "he seems like the devil", a watch "because he was always watching the time to make sure he got finished before anybody came home", and a tie "because he was always dressed up. During this activity, it became clear that the perpetrator had a bald spot on the top of his head and a mustache although neither physical feature had been mentioned previous to the completion of this exercise. These physical features became important jumping off points for discussing physical sensations she experienced during the abuse. As you may notice, she also has a downward pointing nose and another upward pointing nose on the perpetrator. When the client is finished building the puppet and processing the building of it, the invitation may be made to talk to the perpetrator symbol (if there's anything the client wishes to say or wishes he had said at the time of the trauma). The last step is to invite the client to manipulate the perpetrator symbol in whatever way he wishes. Some children will jail the perpetrator at this point. Others will "rip" or "cut" off it's eyes, ears, etc. (easy to do with Velcro parts) until only remnants of the perpetrator are left.

Processing Questions:
Describe the person who hurt you.
Which puppet parts were you drawn to?
How is the puppet you've made like the person who hurt you?
How is it different?
What (if anything) would you like to say to it? Do to it?
How did it feel to say(do) what you've been wanting to say to the puppet?

Homework Assignment:
Be sure that the client has manipulated or contained the perpetrator symbol in some way by the end of the session. Say to the client, "I know that sometimes during the week you think about the person who hurt you and get scared all over again. This week when you that person's face comes into your head, practice replacing it with a picture of what we've done today." Have the client report next week on how well they were able to do this.

Special Considerations:
Therapists must be careful when using this intervention, as it encourages the client to act out fantasies related to having power over the perpetrator. This intervention would be contraindicated for the child whose difficulty is that he already acts out his aggressive impulses outside the playroom. This intervention is best suited for clients who are afraid of their perpetrators, almost to the point of paralysis. These children are only able to engage with the perpetrator symbol because it is a playful symbol, it is done in the safe, confined space of the

playroom and they are buffered by the person of the play therapist.

Applications and Modifications:

The "create your own puppet" set can also be used to help a client assess the impact of the trauma on his sense of self by doing a "before, during, after" series of puppets. Begin by having the client create a puppet to represent himself before the abuse began. Then ask the client to change the puppet in some way to reflect "the self" during the time he was traumatized. Finally, have the client change the puppet one more time to reflect the way the child sees himself now that the abuse is over and the healing process has begun.

Skill Building Exercises

(Feelings Identification, Anger Management, Impulse Control, Pro-social Skills)

Taking Your Temperature

Treatment Modality: Individual/Group/Family
Population: Ages 3 to 12
Treatment Phase: Joining/Working Phase

Treatment Goals:
1. To help the client identify his current feeling state
2. To expand the client's feelings vocabulary
3. To help client grasp that several feelings can be experienced simultaneously
4. To give the client a nonverbal way of articulating feelings
5. To help the client practice matching appropriate affect with feelings verbalization

Props:
Doctor's bag or kit
Tongue depressors
Markers

Procedure:
Children who are seen in treatment are often lacking in even a rudimentary understanding of their feelings. Children who hit and hurt may be unable to say that they are angry or don't realize that they are angry until their bodies have already

reacted. Young children tantrum, letting their feelings vent through their physical bodies because they are lacking the words to vent them verbally. Emotional literacy is an important goal for many clients. The first step towards this goal is emotional awareness. Children must be able to check in with themselves and recognized their feelings going on inside. Once they have recognized the feelings, they can impact the resulting behaviors. Since many children come into treatment unable to articulate any feelings or only know basic feeling words like "happy", "mad," and "sad," more complex emotions are often difficult. This activity is a fun, prop-based way of engaging children in feelings exploration while keeping them kinesthetically involved.

Start by talking to the child about going to the doctor. Children go and see a doctor to make sure that they are healthy or to get help when they are sick. Ask the child what doctors do in the examining room. The child may mention things like taking blood pressure, checking reflexes, looking in the child's throat and ears, etc. Eventually the child will talk about taking a temperature. A temperature lets us know that the body is sick and fighting infection. Explain to the child that he is going to be the doctor. The child will get to take the therapist's temperature first. This puts the child in the position of power, while allowing the therapist to model feelings articulation. Tell the child that every doctor carries his/her own bag of instruments. Introduce the doctor's kit that is kept in the playroom, and then tell the child that he will be able to personalize the bag. Give the child between five and fifteen blank tongue depressors, depending on their age. Ask the client to write down all the feelings that he has felt today, one on each tongue depressor. The younger child can draw feeling faces, or the therapist can act as scribe. Usually the child will generate one or two on his own. Then invite the child to figure out what feeling the therapist is showing and write this on a tongue depressor. Once enough feelings have been written on the tongue depressors, the child may store these in the doctor's bag.

© Paris Goodyear-Brown, 2005. All Rights Reserved.

The therapist then role plays a patient coming to see the doctor. Just as a real doctor assesses his patient to determine what is wrong, the child will assess the therapist - only the game will focus on identifying feeling states. The child will choose the tongue depressor out of his bag that matches the therapist's affect.

This child's feelings repertoire can be expanded over several sessions by adding tongue depressors to the bag. After the child has had a chance to be the doctor, the child and therapist switch roles. The child gets an opportunity to practice matching facial affect to feeling words.

Processing Questions:
Which feeling words came the most quickly for you?
Which of your own feelings are the easiest for you to identify?
Which facial expressions (of other people) were the easiest to interpret? Which were the hardest?
Are there times when your facial expression does not match your feelings? Give an example.

Homework Assignment:
Begin to pay more attention to the facial expressions of those around you. Keep a journal. During the next week, if you come across someone and you can't interpret his expression, ask him what he is feeling and write it down in your journal.

Special Considerations:
The youngest children may need to draw picture faces on the tongue depressors. Alternatively, the therapist can act as scribe for the child and write the feeling words. The child could even cut out different facial expressions from magazines and glue them onto the tongue depressors. This technique may not be appropriate for children who do not enjoy role play.

© Paris Goodyear-Brown, 2005. All Rights Reserved.

Applications and Modifications:

This technique is particularly useful with children on the Aspergers-Autism continuum. These children have a great deal of trouble accurately reading and responding to non-verbal cues - especially related to emotions. In a group setting, this intervention offers a fun vehicle for helping these clients practice matching appropriate affect to various feeling states.

Introducing a mirror to the exercise adds another dimension. Clients have an opportunity to assess their own facial expressions for how accurately they portray internal feeling states. To the extent that there is a mismatch between affect and internal state, clients may begin to understand how others misinterpret their communications.

Lastly, this technique can become a non-verbal feelings check-in at the beginning of each session. The therapist hands the bag to the client and says "Take your temperature". The client then rummages through the bag, pulling out as many of the tongue depressors as describe his current feeling states.

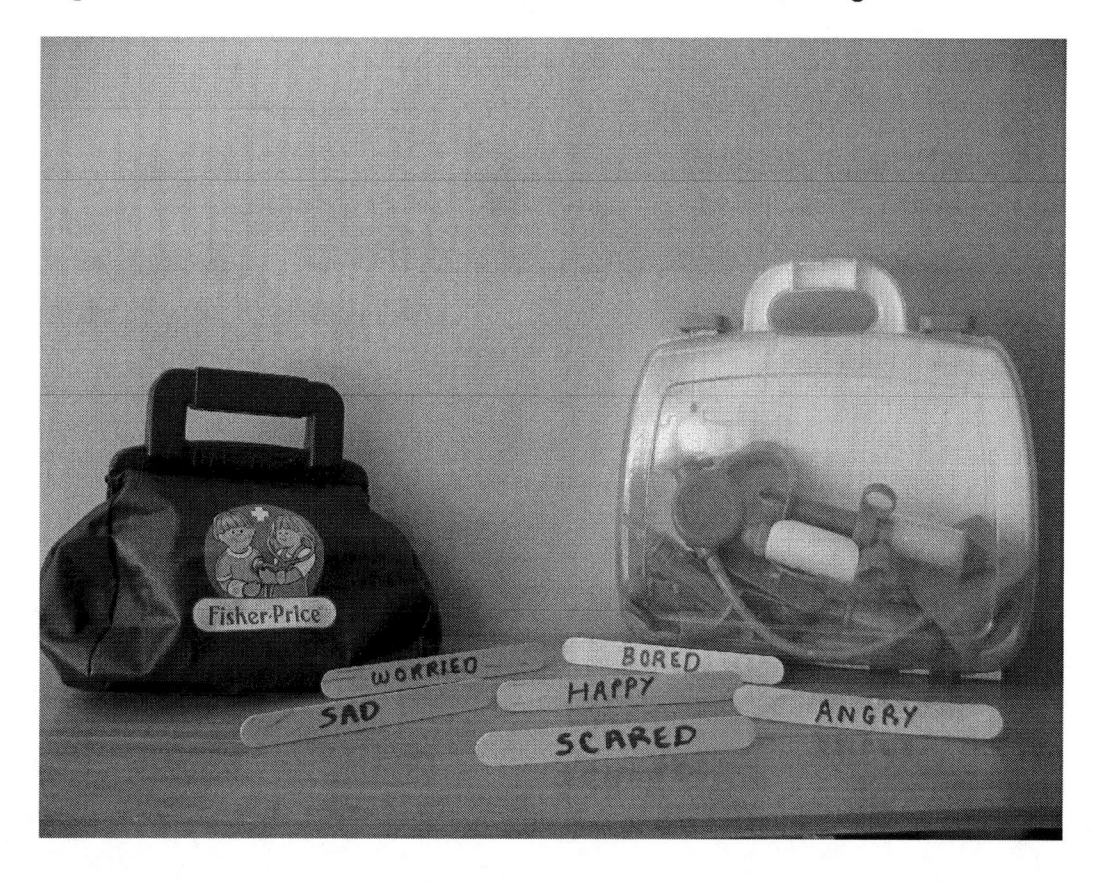

© Paris Goodyear-Brown, 2005. All Rights Reserved.

Inside/Outside Feelings

Treatment Modality: Individual/Group/Family
Population: Ages 6 to 18
Treatment Phase: Working Phase

Treatment Goals:
1. To increase clients' awareness of the image she projects to others
2. To increase clients' awareness of internal feeling states
3. To help client accurately identify and verbalize feeling states

Props:
Manila file folders
Magazines
Scissors
Glue
Markers

Procedure:

Many children referred for treatment have deficits in areas relating to emotional literacy. Children who have externalizing disorders often experience difficulties in peer and family relationships. Often this is due to a mismatch in the client's outward behavior and his internal feeling state. For example, a client might be feeling sad but outwardly engaging in a temper tantrum that looks like rage. The tantrum is not effectively communicating the child's feelings of disappointment and is shutting down the parent's motivation to understand the problem and rectify it. These clients need to explore how others see them to become aware of how their behaviors and demeanor are interpreted by others. At the same time, these clients need to become accurate identifiers and communicators of their feeling states. This activity is a starting point for working on these goals.

Begin by giving the client a blank file folder. Have the client cut out a head and shoulders in the top of the file folder. The file folder effectively becomes a representation of a person. The outside covers are the front and back view of the person's head and shoulders. When the file folder is opened up, the two inside surfaces can represent the hidden or internal life of the client. Ask the client to describe a troublesome situation from the past week. For example, the client goes back and forth between his parents' houses. Mom was in a hurry to get home when she picked the client up from dad's house. The client crossed his arms, stuck out his lip, stomped his feet and refused to get in the car. Have the client describe how he might have looked to a bystander. Instruct the client to draw himself this way on the front. Have the client look at his drawn image and generate some words to describe himself. In this example, the words might be "mad", "stubborn", "mean", "defiant", etc. Then ask the client to try and identify what he was actually thinking and feeling. Thoughts and feelings can be written on the inside of the person. It is sometimes more effective to give the client a stack of magazines at this point

© Paris Goodyear-Brown, 2005. All Rights Reserved.

and ask him to cut out pictures that reflect what he was thinking and feeling on the inside - the stuff that no one else got to see. Latency-age kids and adolescents particularly like to create collages as a way of exploring feelings, thoughts and behaviors. When the client is finished, process the differences between the outside and inside views. Role play with the client what actually happened (the previous example ended in mom angrily dragging the client to the car) and role play with the client verbalizing more of his actual thoughts and feelings to his mom. The mom's role played response will be different based on how the client communicates.

Processing Questions:
Tell me about one conflict that happened this week.
What did your body and face look like during the conflict?
What did you say and do during the conflict?
How did the other person see you during this time?
What were you really thinking and feeling on the inside?
Did you let the other person see any of this?
What could you say and do differently to share what was actually going on inside you?

Homework Assignment:
Encourage the client to spend the time between sessions becoming aware of feelings and thoughts that he may not be sharing when things get hard. Ask him to write these down. At the next session, the client can practice making appropriate verbalizations of some of these internal states. Homework for the next session would be to try verbalizing these new responses in at least one situation during the week.

Special Considerations:
Clients need to become aware of the feelings and thoughts going on inside them when their responses to others are problematic. However, it is very important that the client

practice appropriate verbalizations of these feelings and thoughts in the playroom *before* they attempt this in other environments. The client may *be* smiling but internally *be* thinking "I hate you." If the client believes that he should blurt out the words "I hate you" the next time he finds himself in the described situation, he will only exacerbate the problem. Therefore, appropriate communication skills must *be* taught concurrently with the increasing self-awareness of internal states.

Applications and Modifications:

Toddlers and early pre-school age children may have very little ability to think about their thought processes (meta-cognition). They live in the moment. These children may benefit more from working with a pre-constructed situation than attempting to rehash their own previous life experiences. This is a great age for puppet work. Act out a story with puppets. Invite the client to describe what happened in the story. Take the client through the same steps that would have been completed with the inside/ outside person, but in relation to a character in the puppet story. After the client has guessed at the internal feeling states of the puppet, the client is invited to take the puppet and role play appropriate expression of the feelings.

Pens Up!! Switch!! Draw!!

Treatment Modality: Group/Family
Population: Ages 3 to adult
Treatment Phase: Beginning phase/Working phase

Treatment Goals:
1. To increase the client's self-control
2. To increase immediate compliance with adult requests
3. To increase the client's cooperation skills
4. To assist the client in integrating the feedback of peers

Props:
Blank white paper
Pens
Markers
Crayons

Procedure:
This technique is very useful with groups of children with Attention Deficit Disorder, Oppositional Defiant Disorder, Disruptive Disorder and any other disorder which impedes the

child's ability to self-monitor, comply with directions, and cooperate with peers. It is best to begin by having the group members sit in a circle around a table. Each person is given a blank piece of paper. Each person is asked to choose a color (or marker, crayon, pen). The only qualification is that each group member must choose a different color. This will become important later in the activity. Explain the following directions to the group: "When the therapist says "Pens up!!", each group member must raise his writing utensil high above his head. The therapist will then say, "Draw" and each group member must draw on his own paper (keeping his eyes on his own paper) until the therapist again says "Pens up!!" Points are awarded for prompt compliance with these requests. After all the pens are back up, the therapist will say, "Switch!!" and each group member will move his paper in front of the person to his right. In this way, each paper will be passed around the entire group. By the end of the exercise, each group member will have contributed some kind of drawing to each piece of paper.

After the directions have been explained, allow the group to have one or two practice turns. It may become a contest to see who can put his pen up the fastest once the directive has been given. Choose in advance what sort of token will be handed out for quick compliance. Tokens may only be needed for the first few rounds, as the compliance often becomes a competition between group members and doesn't need external rewards. Once the papers have gone all the way around the circle and come back to the person who first drew on them, stop the process.

Direct each client to make up a story about his drawing. The story must include a beginning, a middle and an end and it must integrate all the parts of the picture. This may be difficult for some clients who may be frustrated by what other group members drew on their paper. Indeed, most clients start out their drawings with an intention in mind. Then they pass their papers off and their peers may add elements to the drawings that change the original intent. (This technique is often a good test of a client's frustration tolerance). A client may begin drawing a house and then the peer next to him scribbles a tornado all over the paper. The story that the original artist creates must incorporate these disparate elements.

Processing Questions:

How easy or hard was it for you to comply when the therapist said "Pens Up"?
How did it feel to have to stop drawing even if you weren't finished?
What part of you overruled the part that wanted to keep drawing?
How did it feel to get your paper back and see what other people had drawn?
Were you able to create a story that combined all the elements of your picture? What was that like?
How can you apply what you've done here when playing with your peers?

Homework Assignment:

Encourage the client to approach a group of kids on the playground or in his neighborhood. Challenge him to find a way to join in the play. Remind him that it may take a minute to find his place among what the children are already doing. Another assignment would be to choose one direction that is often given by the client's teacher. Invite the child to pretend that when the teacher gives that direction, it is a game (like Pens Up!!) that requires immediate compliance. Talk with the teacher and arrange a system of immediate rewards for immediate compliance with this one request.

Special Considerations:
Some children in treatment are too volatile to tolerate "sharing" their pictures with other group members. Children must be carefully screened for appropriateness and frustration tolerance before this technique is introduced. This technique is useful even with very young children who may not be able to draw clear figures yet, as it is free-flowing. Children who come from extreme trauma situations will often project their traumas onto the story that they creates. Clinicians should be prepared to process traumatic stories if necessary.

Applications and Modifications:
This technique can be used as an assessment technique. As mentioned above, the stories generated after the art portion is completed are projective in nature. This activity can be done at the beginning of a new group, during the working phase and again at the end. Clinicians may assess for changes in the both the content of the story and the client's ability to easily integrate the contributions of others.

Extinguish the Behavior

Treatment Modality: Individual/Group/Family
Population: Ages 5 to 15
Treatment Phase: Working phase

Treatment Goals:
1. To help the client confront problematic behavior patterns
2. To equip the client with strategies to avoid engagement in the problematic behavior
3. To give the client a sense of eradicating the problematic behavior
4. To generate and practice a pro-social replacement behavior

Props:
White board
Dry erase markers
Toy fire extinguisher
Paper
Markers/crayons

© Paris Goodyear-Brown, 2005. All Rights Reserved.

Procedure:

The first step in changing a negative behavior is being aware that the behavior is negative. However, therapists don't get very far when they begin treatment by confronting the child with all the behaviors that need to change. This exercise allows for an indirect route to the same end.

The therapist begins by dividing the dry erase board into six sections. The therapist draws six small pictures, three positive or pro-social behaviors and three negative or antisocial behaviors. The six should be randomly placed on the board. Tell the client that you are going to play a game in which the client has to guess which behaviors on the board should be "extinquished". Ask the child if he knows what this big word means. Older kids will have the answer and younger kids may have a vague association with a fire extinguisher. Show the client the pretend fire extinguisher. Have the client describe what he knows about how they work or why they are used. A connection can then be made between a fire that ends up destroying everything if left unchecked and a behavior that may end up destroying a friendship, getting privileges taken away, etc. Have the client aim the extinguisher at the pictures of behaviors that should be erased. Choosing the correct behavior earns a point in the game. The therapist may wish to shape the number of points needed to win based on the client's accuracy at discriminating between positive and negative behaviors. When water from the extinguisher hits the picture on the whiteboard it begins to run. Have the client use a paper towel or eraser to finish removing each picture. The client then draws a replacement behavior in the spot where the fist picture had been. When the game is finished, the client is invited to draw the pictures for the next round and have the therapist guess. After any initial resistance to addressing negative behaviors has been diminished through game play, it is likely that the child will draw pictures of negative behaviors in which he engages.

© Paris Goodyear-Brown, 2005. All Rights Reserved.

Processing Questions:
What is a pro-social or positive behavior?
What is an anti-social or negative behavior?
How did you decide which pictures to erase?
How did you figure out what pictures to draw in the place of the ones you erased?

Homework Assignment:
Invite the parent into the room to watch the client play the game. Encourage the client and parent to play a simplified version of this game at home with paper and pencil. The negative pictures can be erased and the child earns points for correct discrimination. These can be traded in for a prize.

Special Considerations:
This is an initial introduction to the concepts of positive and negative behavior. The client may end up admitting verbally that he actually engages in this kind of behavior, but that is not the goal. In fact, personalizing the behavior during the initial phase of treatment may increase resistance. The goal is for the client to attain competence at discriminating between various kinds of behavior.

Applications and Modifications:
This game can be especially fun in a group setting. Divide the group into two teams, increase the number of pictures on the board and allow the teams to talk freely together to decide which behaviors need to be extinguished. Each team earns points for correct discrimination. There are also more ideas available to the team when the time comes to draw pictures of replacement behaviors.

© Paris Goodyear-Brown, 2005. All Rights Reserved.

Mad Maracas

Treatment Modality: Individual/Group/Family
Population: Ages 3 to 14
Treatment Phase: Working Phase

Treatment Goals:
1. To help the client correctly identify feelings of anger
2. To help the client understand the continuum of anger and how it escalates
3. To help the client appropriately express anger early in the escalation pattern

Props:
Maracas of varying sizes and shapes
Dried Beans
Rice
Empty containers
Sticks

Procedure:
Many clients struggle with problematic anger reactions. When a child is angry, the anger will be expressed behaviorally until the client learns to communicate effectively with spoken language. Child clients also lack understanding about the nuances of anger, how angry feelings can vary in intensity and

© Paris Goodyear-Brown, 2005. All Rights Reserved.

quality (i.e. disappointment vs. annoyance vs. rage), and how to catch the anger escalation early in the process. This activity is meant to help educate children about these processes and allow them to ultimately practice appropriate verbal expressions of anger. Begin by showing the client the collection of maracas. The client's focus is more likely to be extended if there are many maracas to manipulate. These can be purchased inexpensively through mail order catalogues.

Invite the client to choose two maracas and shake them. Have the client shake them hard and then gently, creating both loud and soft sounds. Explain that our anger is like the sounds made by the maracas. Introduce the client to the anger continuum. (This can be done through use of a thermometer or volcano metaphor.) Give an example like this: "One day you wake up really wanting to wear your red shirt, but it is in the laundry. You feel disappointed." Write down the word "disappointed" at the bottom of the thermometer or volcano. "Then you go into the kitchen for breakfast, pour a bowl of cereal and find that your sister finished off the milk. You feel irritated. Then you get on the bus, but someone is sitting in your favorite seat. You feel annoyed. When you get to school, you have trouble with your first math problem. You feel frustrated. Then Johnny rolls his eyes at you and you punch him." Explain that the anger that was behind the choice to punch Johnny had begun to build early in the morning. Take the client through another example, but allow the client to fill in the blank, "You feel _____" after each part of the story by shaking the maracas. The client will shake them hard if that part of the story would make them really angry and more softly for feelings of irritation, annoyance, etc. Help the client become aware of what happens in his body when anger is building up. Role play situations in which the client becomes angry. Often, children become angry when someone else is doing something (like laughing at them, hitting, poking, or making loud noise) around them or to them. The therapist plays the role of the person engaged in annoying behavior. At first, the client only has to shake the maracas to make the

© Paris Goodyear-Brown, 2005. All Rights Reserved.

therapist stop whatever she is doing. The client begins to feel powerful. He shakes the maracas and the anger inducing behavior stops. This increase the client's motivation to practice the next step. Next, the therapist helps the client design verbalizations to replace the shaking of the maracas. One example is "I feel angry when you laugh at me." Another example is "I don't like it when you use my pencil without asking." Help the client practice making these verbalizations and talk about real life situations where these statements would be useful.

Processing Questions:
What are some things that make you angry?
What are some words you know that describe anger?
Are you always "a lot" angry or are you sometimes "a little bit" angry?
How did it feel to shake the maracas and have the other person stop the annoying behavior?
What are some words you can use to get people to stop doing things that bother you?

Homework Assignment:
If the parent is not already in the room, invite her in. Have the client show the parent the degrees of anger through shaking the maracas with different amounts of vigor. Tell the parent that the client is working on using his words to express anger. Design a chart that allows the parent to positively reinforce the client whenever he uses appropriate words to express anger. Have the family bring the chart back next week for troubleshooting and celebration.

Special Considerations:
At the beginning of treatment, many child clients are defensive about their anger issues. By the time they come to the playroom, they have been criticized repeatedly for their

problematic expressions of anger. They may believe that they are "bad" when they show anger. The challenge for the therapist is to help the client learn and practice more effective tools for expressing anger without shaming them. Children may be less resistant to working with stories in which other characters get into anger-inducing situations. Bibliotherapy materials (reading a story to the child and letting him shake the maracas at various points in the story to reflect the level of anger he believes the characters are feeling) and puppet work can both be helpful modalities for anger exploration.

Applications and Modifications:

The client's investment in the practice of new anger expression skills may increase if the client is encouraged to make his own instrument. The simplest way to do this is to give the client two empty plastic eggs and some fillers (i.e. dried beans, rice, sand, etc.). The client can easily make several different shaker eggs that will give off sounds that reflect varying degrees of anger. The client can take the new instruments home and continue his exploration there. This technique is also fun to do in a group. In a group setting, members can experiment with how much noise (reflecting varying degrees of anger) they can generate separately and as a group.

Fire-Breathing Dragons

Treatment Modality: Individual/Group/Family
Population: Ages 5 to adult
Treatment Phase: Working Phase

Treatment Goals:
1. To educate the client about anger escalation patterns
2. To help the client identify situations in which the client responds with anger
3. To help the client identify problematic anger expressions
4. To equip the client with alternative strategies for expressing anger appropriately

Props:
Construction paper
Markers
Dragon puppet(s)
Toy dragons

Procedures:
Children love fairy tales and magical, mystical creatures. Boys, especially, love dragons and the fire-breathing dragon can be

effectively used as a metaphor for a client's own anger expression.

Begin by showing the client the dragon puppet or collection of dragon symbols. I have several dragon puppets in the playroom, ranging in size from finger puppets to hand puppets to a dragon puppet the size of most four year olds. I also have two and three headed dragons that are often used in sandtray work. A collection of this kind allows the client to choose the dragon symbol that resonates with him. Ask the client what he knows about dragons. More than likely, he will volunteer the information that dragons breathe fire. Once this has been established, ask what the fire does. It destroys things by burning them up. Make the comparison between when a dragon breathes fire on something and when one person spews angry words at another. Using orange and yellow construction paper, cut out jagged shapes that look like fiery breath. Ask the client to write down some angry words that he has heard one person say to another. This can be repeated until there are many pieces of fire shaped construction paper with inappropriate anger expressions on them. Encourage the client to think beyond words to actions and to generate angry actions that one person does to another. These are written on more pieces of construction paper. Ask the client how other people might respond to these angry words and actions. Give the client an experience of how negatively these anger expressions can end up by allowing the client to "be" the dragon puppet while the therapist chooses another puppet. One by one, the fiery phrases are held up in front of the dragon's mouth. The client makes the anger expressions while the puppet held by the therapist is blasted by the "heat", causing this puppet to run away or be destroyed. The fire shaped paper pieces can then be tied to treatment goals regarding behaviors that need to be decreased. Over the next few sessions, each of the problematic anger expressions represented by a piece of fiery breath can be replaced with a positive anger expression. The client helps to generate the replacement behavior or verbalization and then practices the new strategy by having the dragon puppet engage in the new behavior. The therapist's puppet will respond to the new behavior by remaining in relationship with the dragon and modeling pro-social interactions.

Processing Questions:
What was it like to be the dragon?
Do you think the dragon ever feels lonely? In what way?
What are some angry things people say to each other?
How do people respond when someone blasts them with anger?
What are some other ways to share feelings of anger without making people run away?

Homework Assignment:
Have the client choose one of the fiery breath papers to work on. Help the client generate a replacement strategy in session. The client writes this alternative anger expression on the back side of the paper shaped like fire. The client then takes this one replacement strategy home and is instructed to practice this strategy one time everyday. A positive reinforcement chart can be designed to help the parent affirm the client's pro-social practice of appropriate anger expressions.

Special Considerations:
Children who are too young to write may draw pictures on the fire shaped pieces of construction paper. In order to decrease a client's initial resistance to dealing with his own anger issues, it may be beneficial to use bibliotherapy materials to show positive and negative expressions of anger. A recent animated film that has become part of our childrens' cultural context is "Shrek". There is a fire-breathing lady dragon in this movie. At one point in the movie, she ends up all alone because she attempts to use her anger to make others do what she wants. Her later pro-social interactions give her a friendship circle.

Applications and Modifications:

This technique can be used to help a family system look at the difficulties that anger expressions create for the family. Anger that is being inappropriately expressed by a child client has often been modeled by other people in that child's family. In family therapy, each family member can write down two to three typical responses to anger. These can be role played using the dragon puppet and others chosen by the family. As it becomes clear that these problematic expressions of anger only exacerbate the conflict in the family system, the family can begin to generate and practice pro-social expressions of anger using the same puppets.

Ants in My Pants

Treatment Modality: Individual/Group/Family
Population: Ages 4 to 12
Treatment Phase: Working phase

Treatment Goals:
1. To catalog the client's typical hyperactive behaviors
2. To draw connections between hyperactive behavior and the situations in which the impulsive behaviors happen
3. To teach coping skills to de-escalate hyperactivity and psycho-motor agitation
4. To practice newly acquired coping skills through role play

Props:
Ant stickers
White paper
Markers
Construction paper
Staples
Ant finger puppets

Procedure:

This technique was designed for children who have been diagnosed with ADD. Many parents and teachers who have children with ADD characterize these children as having "ants in their pants". Moreover, the metaphor is silly enough to engage children, particularly elementary school age and latency age boys.

Begin by asking the child if he has ever had ants in his pants. The child will probably giggle and say "no". Ask him what it would feel like to have ants in his pants. Would it be easy to sit still with ants in your pants? Would it be easy to pay attention to what a teacher were saying if you had ants in your pants? The answer to both of these questions is no. Ask the child to draw a self-portrait on a sheet of very large construction paper. Then make a pair of pants out of the construction paper and staple them onto the self-portrait. If you staple the sides of the pants and the bottom, you end up with what is essentially a pocket. Introduce the ant stickers and a stack of thin strips of white paper. Have the client attach an ant sticker to a strip of paper and then write out or draw one way that he might act like he has ants in his pants. Some possibilities that might be generated are, "When I tap my pencil on the desk over and over," or "when I sit on my knees in my seat instead of on my bottom," or "when I pass notes with Sally". Allow the child to exhaust the number of hyperactive behaviors of which he is aware. If there are other problematic behaviors that the teacher or parent has made the therapist aware of, the therapist can introduce these as other behaviors that often make children look like they have ants in their pants. Depending on the defensiveness of the child, he may be able to own some of these behaviors that he did not originally volunteer. As each ant strip is generated, the client can fold it up and put it in the pants "pocket" that has been stapled to the self-portrait. This part of the exercise may take the entire session. Even if there is time left over, the therapist may choose to put this activity aside and continue it

© Paris Goodyear-Brown, 2005. All Rights Reserved.

next week. When the child returns, the therapist brings out the self-portrait with the ants in the pants. The child is invited to pull out one ant strip at a time. If the child pulls out a strip that says, "I kick my feet out in front of me a lot and get in trouble when Sally complains about it," it is the therapist's job to help the client generate a coping strategy to mitigate this behavior. The coping strategy for dealing with one "ant in the pants" might be a self-talk statement like "Stop and Think," a deep breathing exercise, or a practical step like moving the client's desk to a different place in the classroom. As each coping skill is generated, it can be written or drawn on the back of the original ant strip.

It is not enough, however, to talk about coping strategies. The child must have an opportunity to practice them. This is where the fingerpuppet ants come in handy (ant fingerpuppets can be purchased from FolkManis and Manhatten Toys). It can be fun to put several of them in a pair of doll's pants, then have the child pull out one at a time and have the ant puppet practice one of the coping strategies. In this way, each of the coping strategies can be practiced using a fingerpuppet. Once the strategies have been practiced, the therapist may ask the client if he would like to put on a puppet play for the parents showing the new coping strategies that he has learned. In this way the learning is reinforced.

Processing Questions:

What does it feel like to have ants in your pants?
Which of the "ants in your pants" behaviors do you most want to change?
What would your body/behavior look like if the ants went away?
Which of the coping strategies that we practiced is the easiest for you to do? Which is the hardest? Why?

Homework Assignment:

The activity is most effective when parents are involved and understand both the concept of the ants in the pants and the

© Paris Goodyear-Brown, 2005. All Rights Reserved.

coping strategies that the child is practicing. Homework can then *be* assigned in which the parent is given a sheet of ant stickers to take home (a positive behavior chart can also be designed). The child's job is to implement the coping strategies at home and the parent's job is to look for them and reward each attempt to utilize a coping strategy with an ant sticker. Have them talk next session about how this assignment went.

Special Considerations:

Children have various idiosyncratic fears and may have a fear of ants that would get in the way of the work. As always, the therapist's discretion must *be* used in assessing how easily any given client will embrace this particular metaphor. Some children may need hand puppets that symbolize the actual characters in a situation to create an effective role play instead of the ant finger puppets.

Applications and Modifications:

One fun way to modify the activity for a group setting is to have one member of the group lay down on butcher paper, have another group member draw the outline, another cut out large paper ants and another make the pants to staple on the figure. Then each group member generates one or two ways that they behave as if they have "ants in their pants". After all the ants have been put on the pants, group members take turns chosing one at a time. All group members help generate and role play coping strategies to deal with the hyperactive behavior.

© Paris Goodyear-Brown, 2005. All Rights Reserved.

On the Other Hand...

Treatment Modality: Individual/Group/Family
Population: Ages 7 to 18
Treatment Phase: Working phase

Treatment Goals:
1. To increase the client's perspective taking skills
2. To increase the client's success in social situations
3. To increase the client's problem solving skills

Props:
8 1/2 x 11 inch pieces of felt
A hole puncher
Yarn or string
A pair of gloves
Permanent marker

Procedure:
Many of the children seen in treatment have impairments in their ability to take the perspective of others. This deficit makes it difficult for these children to successfully navigate social situations. Often the child who is unable to engage in

© Paris Goodyear-Brown, 2005. All Rights Reserved.

perspective taking will assume that his solution is "the right" solution or "the only" solution, when multiple solutions may be possible. Some clients, based on early negative tapes, will perceive others as "out to get them". They will ascribe negative connotations to the actions of others. Let's look at an example. An 11 year old boy named Jonathan has gotten his lunch and is looking for a place to sit. There are two boys whom he would like to get to know. However, as he approaches them, he notices that their heads are together, whispering. Jonathan immediately assumes that the boys are talking about him, feels mad or ashamed, and responds by walking away and eating lunch by himself. If Jonathan had been able to entertain more than one possible explanation for this behavior before making a decision about how to respond he may have ended up making two new friends that day. The intent behind this exercise is to help clients like Jonathan entertain at least two alternative explanations, solutions, choices, etc. at a time.

Begin by having the client trace his left hand on a piece of felt. Fold this piece in half and cut two identical copies of the left hand. Repeat this activity for the right hand. Punch holes in the edges and sew the two halves together with yarn or twine. These become makeshift gloves for the child. Ask the client to describe a social situation that had a negative outcome. Many of our clients with externalizing behavior disorders have daily fights with their peers. Help the client choose one such incident. Get the client to specifically process how he perceived the actions of the other party. Then have him write or draw this perception on the left hand glove. Next, ask the client to try to put himself in the other person's place. This client is often sure that their perception is the correct one, so the therapist must challenge him to see other possibilities. In the example of Jonathan and the two boys at lunch, it is possible that the boys were whispering about a cool toy that one of them brought to school. Have the client write or draw this alternate explanation for the other party's behavior on the other "glove". The activity should be a launching pad for helping children practice perspective taking.

© Paris Goodyear-Brown, 2005. All Rights Reserved.

Help the client see how taking a new perspective on the situation can change his behavior.

Processing Questions:
What do you tend to think of first when you approach a new person?
What kind of behavior makes you the most angry at others?
Talk about one time that a friend misunderstood you.
Why do you think this happened?
Talk about another situation from your past. How would looking at "the other hand" have helped you?

Homework Assignment:
Invite the client to practice this new perspective taking task one time during the next week. Explain to the client that he is likely to be in an uncomfortable situation or disagreement with peers over the next week. Ask the client to try recognizing his own perspective and then take the other person's perspective before responding to the situation. Report back during the next session.

Special Considerations:
The most important consideration here is developmental. This technique is inappropriate for toddlers and early pre-schoolers, as egocentricity characterizes these developmental stages. They may not yet have developed the capacity for other-centered thought and introducing this activity might set the child up for failure. Also, clients may need help identifying their negative tapes or articulating the false motives that they often ascribe to others. An example of this would be the belief, "They don't like me", or "They think I'm stupid."

Applications and Modifications:

This technique has a multitude of applications. It was originally intended for clients who have difficulty in social relationships due to aggression resulting from the misinterpretion of the motives of others. This technique can be used to help a client examine several different solutions to a difficult problem. The activity could be altered so that clients write their negative thoughts down and stuff them inside one of the felt gloves and then generates replacement thoughts for the other glove. Several replacement thoughts could be stored inside the other felt glove and taken home. The client can then pull them out whenever he needs a reminder of the replacement thoughts he generated in session. Children who struggle with shyness could also benefit from this intervention. The therapist could ascertain what the child normally tells himself when he considers approaching another person. Accurate possibilities for how the client might be received should be explored, written up and put inside the glove. The client can then practice having his traditional response, but can also practice thinking, "but on the other hand...." Through perspective taking, the shy child can find a way to reach out to peers.

What's Bugging You?

Treatment Modality: Individual/Group/Family
Population: Ages 5 to 12
Treatment Phase: Working phase

Treatment Goals:
1. To help the client explore angry feelings
2. To increase the client's understanding of the connection between feelings, thoughts and situations
3. To give the client anger reduction strategies

Props:
2 each of several different kinds of pretend bugs
2 small sandtrays
A can of air freshener
Various bug puppets or finger puppets

Procedure:
Many of the children we see have difficulty dealing with their anger. This technique is a playful way to allow clients to catalogue the situations they respond to with anger, help them explore the thoughts generated by these situations and then change these thoughts. This activity is empirically informed, in that it takes tenants of tried and true cognitive-behavioral

theory and practice and delivers it to the client in a play therapy vehicle. First, the therapist shows the client the "bag of bugs". You may want to have a variety of bugs, some that are clearly harmless and pretend, others that are dangerous and "gross looking" (these will interest many latency-age male clients). Introduce the first sandtray and invite the client to play a game of hide-and-go-seek. The therapist hides the bugs in the sand and the child hunts for them. Each time the child finds a bug, they verbalize one situation that makes them angry. For example, a child may say, "I get angry when I get an answer wrong at school". Introduce the second sandtray. In this one, the therapist and client put a sign that says "thoughts". The child may want to draw a picture of a brain or a person thinking. Explain to the child that our thoughts about a situation can often make us feel a certain way. For example, in the situation above "giving a wrong answer at school", the client thinks, "Everyone will think I'm stupid," and then he feels angry. If the thought is changed, the resulting feeling will change. If the client dug up a ladybug in the first tray, he rifles through the bag of bugs until he finds another ladybug. Then he puts this second bug into the "thoughts" sandtray as he pinpoints the thought or thoughts he has in the anger inducing situation.

    Then the can of "bugspray" is introduced. This can be any kind of aerosol can that has been wrapped in a piece of blank construction paper before the session starts. Explain to the client that just like bugspray kills bugs, new healthy thoughts can "kill" the unhealthy thoughts that make us angry. Encourage the client to decorate the label of the can that will "kill" the unhealthy thoughts. The client and therapist generate replacement thoughts and the client says them out loud as he sprays the bug with the can. After each replacement thought is spoken aloud, check in with the client about what kind of feeling this new thought engenders.

Processing Questions:
Describe the most common situations in which you get angry.
What are you thinking when you get angry?
Can you think a new thought to replace the angry one? What is it?
How does this new thought make you feel?

Homework Assignment:
More than likely, this exercise has revolved around everyday situations in which the client becomes angry. Encourage the client to pick just one situation that may come up this week. Tell the client to practice the new thought in this situation and to check in with himself about how he feels as he uses the new thought. The therapist will want to help the client write down or draw out a symbolic representation of the replacement thought for this one situation. The client can hang this thought on his wall, bathroom mirror, or refrigerator. Enlist the parent to help the client practice the replacement thought each morning in the mirror before leaving for school.

Special Considerations:
The youngest clients will be unable to participate effectively in this activity due to their inability to engage in metacognition-(their ability to think about their own thoughts). However, as the angry situations are put in the sandtray, it becomes easier for children to externalize their accompanying thought life. Children may complete the activity with more ease if they first see the therapist model an example of an angry situation, the underlying anger inducing thought, and the replacement thought. It is also important that the client have ownership of the replacement thought. The therapist may be able to generate five replacement statements, but if the client doesn't believe any of them, they will be of little use. Be sure the client chooses one that actually decreases his level of anger upon verbalization of the new thought.

© Paris Goodyear-Brown, 2005. All Rights Reserved.

Applications and Modifications:

While the metaphor being used here is "what's bugging you?" as a way of looking at anger, other materials could be used to help clients explore this same CBT process with other feelings. For example, the therapist could cut "tears" out of blue construction paper, hide those in the sand and talk about situations that make a client feel sad. Other symbols could be used with feelings of anxiety, worry, nervousness, etc.
This technique is easily modified for use with groups or families. One interesting dynamic that can sometimes be seen when cognitive-behavioral work is done in a family setting is that several family members may struggle with the same irrational thoughts or beliefs. The parent may have modeled the beliefs or thoughts unwittingly to the child. Doing this activity in a family setting allows all family members to learn from one another and to work together to change faulty beliefs that may extend throughout the whole family system.

Treat 'Em With Kid Gloves

Treatment Modality: Individual/Family
Population: Ages 6 to 15
Treatment Phase: Working phase

Treatment Goals:
1. To help the client take another person's point of view
2. To help the client attend to the physical relational cues given by others
3. To increase the client's number of pro-social encounters
4. To assist the client in integrating the feedback of peers

Props:
A pair of gloves
Permanent marker

Procedure:
Many of the children seen in treatment have impairments in their ability to process and correctly interpret the non-verbal cues of others, particularly those on the Aspergers/Autism continuum. Even when these children can process the non-

© Paris Goodyear-Brown, 2005. All Rights Reserved.

verbal content of others, they seldom let this impact their behavioral response to their peers. These clients need to be given the rudimentary set of skills that most people take for granted. The phrase "treat them with kid gloves" has come to mean that a particular person needs to be treated carefully or with extra gentleness. This is actually a pretty good way to treat everyone. Explain this metaphor to the child. Tell the child that there are certain behaviors we can observe, questions we can ask and things we can do that will help us treat everyone carefully. Explain that the child is going to make his own set of kid gloves during the session.

Begin by inviting the child to choose a pair of gloves. It is most empowering if the therapist has several pairs of gloves to choose from. Many thrift stores sell used gloves inexpensively. Clinicians can also raid their family coat closets. The choices should vary in colors, sizes and fabrics. After the child has chosen a pair of gloves, ask him to describe what he notices first whenever he approaches someone new. Some kids may talk about clothing, others may talk about hair, but the truth is that these children notice very little about other people and tend to focus on specific details, like a necklace. These kids are unlikely to notice aspects of another person that relate to affect. Therefore, the first step is to educate clients about how to read non-verbals. Each non-verbal that the clinician covers is written on one of the fingers of the glove to help remind the child to look for this piece of body language when talking to people. For example, the first step may be to look at the person's mouth - are they smiling, frowning, etc. The child would then write "look at the mouth" or maybe just "mouth" on the first finger of the glove. Another step in assessing non-verbals might be to make eye contact with them and assess what is seen there. Therefore, the child would write on the second finger "eye contact".

The reminders written on each glove may vary from client to client, depending on each child's skill deficits. For children with poor boundaries, the very first finger may need to say "arms length" or "stop" to remind a child to stop an arm's

© Paris Goodyear-Brown, 2005. All Rights Reserved.

length away from someone while completing the rest of their non-verbal assessment. For children who get into trouble for joining a group inappropriately (like many children with ADHD), the first finger may need to say "Look first" to teach the child to ask himself what the other person is already doing. Then the child can match his method of joining to the other person's activity. The gloves might also list behaviors that the child can do to increase the likelihood of success in social encounters. For example, the first finger could say, "Smile". The second finger would read, "Say hello." The third finger would read, "Ask to join them." Each of the "steps" these clients to go through are accomplished by typical children quickly and naturally in any encounter with a new person. However, children whose disorder includes non-verbal learning disabilities need didactic teaching on discrete interpersonal skills. They also need lots and lots of practice. Therefore, after the gloves are complete, have the client wear the gloves while practicing the skills with you in role play.

Processing Questions:
When you approach someone new, what's the first thing you notice?
What is the first step (listed on your gloves) to help you look carefully at someone?
Which of the skills listed on your gloves will be the hardest for you to do? Why?
Which will be the easiest? Why?

Homework Assignment:
After practicing in the playroom, invite the child to choose one person with whom he already has a good relationship. This will set the client up for success. Instruct him to follow the steps on his gloves to "assess" this person before making an approach. Ask the client to do this several times with the

© Paris Goodyear-Brown, 2005. All Rights Reserved.

same person over the course of a week. Have the client report back at the beginning of the next session.

Special Considerations:
Children with severe deficits in reading affective cues, may need to start very slowly. Each session can be used to teach one step, write it on the glove, wear the gloves and practice the skill. The homework assignment would be likewise modified so that each week the skill covered in that week would be practiced with a safe person outside of the therapy room.

Applications and Modifications:
While this technique was originally designed to help clients assess and interpret non-verbal cues such as affect, pitch, tone, body posture, etc., it could be modified to cover any sort of skill set. Children with ADHD typically need some didactic training and practice of impulse control skills, problem solving skills, etc. This technique could easily be adapted for that population. Each of the fingers of the glove would reflect an impulse control skill, such as "Stop and Think", "Take a Deep Breath", "Look ahead" and so forth. The child with ADHD would then wear the gloves (so that when they reach out to touch something or someone they have the visual reminder) while practicing these impulse control skills in session.

Exercises for Building Self-Esteem

Fingerprint Friends

Treatment Modality: Individual/Group/Family
Population: Ages 3 to 18
Treatment Phase: Working
Treatment Goals:
1. To increase the client's positive self-esteem
2. To increase the client's sense of competence
3. To increase the client's positive self-talk
4. To combine visual cues with positive self-talk statements

Props:
White paper
Ink pads (multiple colors)
Construction paper
Baby powder
PlayDoh

Procedure:
Fingerprints are a wonderful way to talk about the uniqueness and value of each individual. A child instinctually enjoys making handprints and footprints. It is a way of leaving a stamp of the self that children find very satisfying. This activity builds on these natural interests. Begin with PlayDoh. Give the child

a small portion of PlayDoh and ask her to flatten it like a pancake. Invite the child to make a fingerprint in the PlayDoh. The therapist makes her own print and then asks the child to compare them. In what ways are they the same? In what ways are they different? Inform the child that no two fingerprints are exactly alike. Each person is unique and different from everyone else. This is cause for celebration. A great bibliotherapy material to read with this activity is Todd Parr's book, It's O.K. to be Different. Ask the client to talk about the ways that she is different from other people. Next, introduce the various pads of ink and clean white paper. Ed Emberley's book on Fingerprint Art is a wonderful resource to use during this activity. Let the client choose which colors to use for making fingerprints. Let the client create fingerprint art. Caterpillars, chicks, people, buildings, clouds, etc. can all be made from fingerprints. Have the client write down one special thing about herself next to each completed piece of fingerprint art. The client may end up with a whole set of pieces of fingerprint art. These can be bound into book form. The client can then create a title that reflects his uniqueness and decorate the cover.

Processing Questions:

Do we all have fingerprints? Are they all the same or are they different from each other? How is this like people?
What are some things that make you special?
How are you different or unique from others?
What are some positive things that you can say about yourself?

Homework Assignment:

If the parent has not been conjointly involved in the activity, invite her in at the end of the session. Explain the book and the concept of uniqueness to the parent. Ask the parent to read the book to the child each night before bedtime in between sessions. Invite the child and caregiver to add to the book by creating more fingerprint art (and more positive self-talk statements) at home together.

Special Considerations:
Some children are uncomfortable with using expressive materials. They do not want to get "messy". Be sure to have a smock and hand wipes available to mitigate this reaction in certain children.

Applications and Modifications:
This activity is usually done with pads of ink and white paper. However, darker construction paper can be used if the child or family wishes to use baby powder instead of ink. The fingerprints would then show up as white prints on a darker background. This activity could piggy-back off the attachment focused activity "Powder Prints", described in this book. In a group or family setting, each member can create different fingerprint creatures, write down the accompanying positive self-statement and cut them out. Once the creatures are arranged together, discussion center around how people can be valued for their individuality while still getting along with others. It is also fun in a group setting to give each client a certain color of ink and have all group members create pictures or creatures together, each contributing fingerprints in her particular color of ink. In this way, all members maintain their individuality and contribute uniquely to the beauty of the finished product.

Sandtray Circles

Treatment Modality: Individual/Group/Family
Population: Ages 4 to adult
Treatment Phase: Working phase

Treatment Goals:
1. To increase the client's positive self-esteem
2. To identify social supports for the client
3. To help the client focus on the positive affirmations made by others
4. To help the client internalize these affirmations and integrate them into a positive sense of self

Props:
Sandtray
At least ten miniature chairs
Other sandtray miniatures

© Paris Goodyear-Brown, 2005. All Rights Reserved.

Procedure:

Many children and adolescents who come for treatment are struggling with low self-esteem. These clients are discouraged. They may have internalized negative comments made by others. Perhaps they have fallen short of their own internal performance goals or goals set by others. Likewise, clients who struggle with depression will become hyperfocused on what they consider to be their inadequacies. They begin to lose sight of the positive support networks they can utilize. This activity is designed to give the client an experience of being surrounded by positive voices in an atmosphere of safety and love. The group work technique called "The Love Circle" is the basis for this adaptation. In the Love Circle, one group member sits in the middle with all other group members surrounding them. Each group member takes a turn expressing his or her positive regard for the person in the middle. This may take the form of a compliment. It may be an encapsulation of one of the positive qualities or resiliencies that this client has shown in group. The person in the middle is to receive the praise and warmth of others and simply say "thank you".

In this adaptation, the whole exercise happens within the boundaries of the sandtray. This contained "world" outside of the self decreases the client's resistance to approaching the positive voices of others. Invite the client to choose a sandtray miniature to represent himself in the tray. If previous sandtray work has been done, the client may already have this symbol selected. Have the client place this symbol in the center of the tray. Introduce the client to the range of miniature chairs, stools, rocking chairs, sofas, etc. that have been collected. Invite the client to choose one chair to represent each family member or other supportive person in the client's life. The client may choose a rocking chair for his grandmother because of it's strong association with nurturing. The client may choose a stool for his English teacher, because she sits on a stool in the classroom. Have the client place each chair in a circle around the self-object. Ask the client to visualize a support person in each chair. Ask the client to verbalize one positive thing that the person in the chair says or might say to him. These may be statements like, "I'm so proud of you", "You're a fantastic artist", or simply "I love you." The client or therapist writes each of these statements down on little banners and these banners are posted in the sand behind each chair. Take a picture of the finished tray and give it to the client.

Processing Questions:
Name a person with whom you feel safe. What is one positive thing this person would say about you?
How does it feel to think about the people who care for you? How does it feel to imagine them telling you what they like about you?
Can you picture this finished tray in your head? Can you hear these people's positive messages in you head?

Homework Assignment:
Give the client a copy of the picture of the finished tray. The client can also take home the positive affirmation banners that were created with his tray. The client is instructed to look at the picture and the banners at least once a day between this session and the next.

Special Considerations:
The tragic truth is that many of our clients have very few positive voices in their lives. Indeed, this is often part of the dysfunctional system that has landed them in treatment. If a child is not able to generate more than one or two support people in his life, it is the therapist's voice that will fill the chairs. The child chooses chairs and matches them to positive verbalizations made by the therapist during the course of treatment. These may be statements like, "you are a very thoughtful person", "you are brave", etc.

Applications and Modifications:

This technique is another fun termination activity in group work. Instead of having the children sit in a circle with one in the middle, the group works in the sandtray. Each group member is instructed to choose a chair for himself. The identified member puts his self-object in the tray. Then, each group member takes a turn putting his chair in the sand circle around the center miniature. When the group member places his chair, he says one positive thing to the focal member. Children are more free to give and receive encouragement from each other when eye contact is not forced because some find it intimidating.

Don't Put All Your Eggs in One Basket

Treatment Modality: Individual/Group/Family
Population: Ages 6 to 18
Treatment Phase: Working Phase

Treatment Goals:
1. To increase the client's positive self-talk
2. To help the client discriminate between positive and negative self-talk messages
3. To help the client practice replacing negative messages with positive reframes

Props:
Two to three different kinds of baskets
Plastic egg shells (the kind used for Easter egg hunts)
Paper
Markers

© Paris Goodyear-Brown, 2005. All Rights Reserved.

Procedure:

Clients often come to treatment with an abundance of negative self-talk. Clients may have unconsciously rehearsed these negative self-talk statements so much that they have become integrated into the "truth" about themselves. At some point in the treatment process, most clients need to have some of these negative beliefs about the self challenged. This activity is a kid friendly vehicle for helping a client begin to become aware of her thought life. Moreover, the technique is designed to help the client sort through various thoughts and categorize them as negative or positive. Sometimes children relate more easily to the terms "good" and "bad", "helpful" or "hurtful" than to the words negative and positive.

Begin by displaying three empty baskets and another basket full of brightly colored, hollow plastic eggs. Because a client's thought life often becomes apparent in relation to particular life events, begin by asking the client to describe a particular situation. Have the client write this down or draw a picture of it and put it in an egg. Then ask "What were you thinking when this thing happened?" If the client thought, "They're talking about me. They think I'm a loser. They don't want to play with me.", have the client write each of these thoughts down (one thought per egg) and put them in the second basket. This basket is labeled "First thoughts". The therapist then asks, "On a scale of one to ten, how does each of these thoughts make you feel?" The client writes down a number between one and ten (one being the worst he could feel and ten being the best) and puts this in another egg. These eggs are placed in a basket labeled "Feelings". Ask the client what he is likely to do based on these feelings and thoughts. This behavior is written down in the final egg and put in a basket called "What I Do". Explain the connection between thoughts, feelings and behaviors and help the client understand that feelings and behaviors can be changed if the client's thoughts are changed. Introduce another basket and label it "Changed Thoughts". Have the client go back to the "First

Thoughts" basket and choose one egg. Work together to restructure or replace this thought with a more reasonable or helpful one. Have the client write this down and put it in the basket labeled "changed thoughts". Have the client rate these changed thoughts on the same feelings scale used previously. Help the client make the connection between new thoughts and better feeling states. Finally, repeat the procedure for "New Actions". The child who may have walked away from children who were whispering together (based on a first thought that they were talking about him) may now walk towards those children because he has constructed a new mediating cognition.

This process can be used once a week to deal with a troublesome situation that emerged during the time between sessions. The client will become more and more proficient at walking through the steps of the process. After the client has gained competence in discriminating between irrational thoughts and more helpful restructuring statements, the game can be changed. All the eggs with thoughts inside them are combined into one basket and the client is invited to sort these based on the kinds of feelings they engender and the resulting behaviors that are informed by the thoughts.

Processing Questions:

Describe one thing that happened this week that makes you feel bad.
What happened? What did you think when it happened? How did you feel? How did you respond in the moment?
What else could you think about what happened?
How do your feelings change when you think this new thought?
How would you act differently with these new thoughts and feelings?

Homework Assignment:

Have the client keep a journal of situations that come up over the course of the week that end up making the client feel bad about herself. As the client becomes better at the egg sorting system, this can be translated into a kind of pen and paper thought record. Have the client bring the thought record into treatment each week.

Special Considerations:

The idea that thoughts, feelings and behaviors are all related may be a new one for clients. The eggs allow for a systematic exploration of these relationships. However, as the information may be overwhelming, clinicians may decide to implement smaller pieces of the technique each week. For example, the client may just write down or draw a picture of the problematic situation one week. The next week the client looks at the thoughts she had surrounding this situation. The next week they look at feelings and resulting behaviors. Developmental differences and each client's individual tolerance for the exercise should guide the clinician.

Applications and Modifications:

This technique can be used in group work. Group members can be divided into teams with one team assigned to each basket. One team creates the situation. The second team writes down "First Thoughts" and fills their eggs. The third team generates the numbers to reflect how they think each of the thoughts would make a child feel. The fourth team predicts what a child's resulting behavior might be. The first and second teams can join forces to create "Changed Thoughts" and the process can be repeated.

Geodes

Treatment Modality: Individual/Group/Family
Population: Ages 4 to 18
Treatment Phase: Working Phase

Treatment Goals:
1. To increase client's positive self-esteem
2. To encourage verbalization of positive self-talk statements
3. To increase client's sense of competence

Props:
Geodes (these are rocks that can be ordered from mineral companies or certain mail-order catalogues)

Procedure:
Geodes are wonderful metaphors for the uniquely beautiful make-up of each individual. Geodes all have the same outward appearance. They are fairly plain looking rocks. In fact, it would be difficult to tell one apart from another. Children often feel that there is nothing special about them. "I'm just like everybody else." In this way, a comparison can be made between the outwardly plain rocks and the way that a particular client may feel about himself. Although geodes border on ugly in their outward appearance, they are astonishingly beautiful on

the inside. When a geode is cracked open, a beautiful design of rock crystals is revealed. Give the client his own geode. Invite him to describe it from its outside appearance. Write these descriptive words down. Invite the client to hit it with a hammer. It is optimal to make a clean break down the middle of the geode. Have the client then describe what he sees inside and write these descriptive words down. These two lists might correspond to "How I think the world sees me" and "What's really inside me." Tell the client that for each crystal point inside the geode, he must say one thing he likes about himself, one thing that he is good at, or one thing that others like about him. The client is likely to say that this is impossible as there are so many crystal points inside. Encourage the client to try. Using the geode as a prop, the client is likely to generate many more self affirming statements than he would have otherwise.

Processing Questions:

What does this geode look like from the outside?
What did you find when you opened the geode?
What does this geode look like on the inside?
How do you think others view you from the outside?
How are you different or unique on the inside?
What are you good at? What do you like about yourself?
What do others like about you?

Homework Assignment:

Make a copy of the list of self-esteem affirming statements that the client makes in session. Give the client a copy to take home as well as the geode. Instruct the client to put the geode and the list in a prominent place in his home. Ask the client to read through the list at least once a day between sessions.

Special Considerations:
Clients often have difficulty articulating the positive qualities in themselves. The metaphor of the geode gives permission for the client to talk about his uniqueness. Moreover, the number of crystals within the geode challenge the client to come up with many self-affirming statements. If the client gets stuck, the therapist needs to assist the client by verbalizing the positive traits, behaviors etc. exhibited by the client.

Applications and Modifications:
A family could utilize the geode as a metaphor for all the beautiful things that make them unique. All families share some qualities (i.e. they involve more than one person), but each family has it's own distinctive culture. Family identity can be more deeply experienced as family members ponder what positive qualities each brings to the family as a whole and what positive processes the family as a whole engages in.

Under Attack

Treatment Modality: Individual/Group
Population: Ages 7 to adult
Treatment Phase: Working phase

Treatment Goals:
1. To help the client increase positive self-esteem
2. To help the client pinpoint negative self-talk statements
3. To help the client externalize these statements in order to create replacement statements
4. To help the client practice thought stopping
5. To help the client practice positive self-talk statements

Props:
Castle or fort
Play-Doh
Toothpicks
Construction paper
Weapons
Army stuff (men, tanks, canons, etc.)

Procedure:

This activity is particularly motivating for young and latency age boys. The underlying tenants of Cognitive-Behavioral Therapy (CBT) will be explored and CBT processes applied to clients suffering from low self-esteem (or other faulty thought patterns). The metaphor of the self as a castle or fort under attack will be used through out the exercise.

Begin by having the client choose a fortification. If the therapist has a pre-fabricated castle or fort, the client may choose one of these. The client may prefer to create his own fortress out of blocks, furniture, army figures, etc. The client is then asked to list the thoughts he thinks about himself that make him feel bad. Client or therapist writes these down and tapes each one to a tank, army men, etc. and places the tanks outside of the walls. These serve as visual reminders of the externalized negative self-talk and give the client a sense of the "battle" to be waged between these negative self-talk statements and restructured, positive replacement thoughts. The client is encouraged to develop a strategy for defeating each of the tanks outside the wall. The client may choose a canon inside to blow up the tank, or station a group of guards on a high wall. Help the client create a positive counter statement for each of the negative self-talk statements. These can be written up on banners and placed as flags on the walls of the battlements. Statements can be written on construction paper, cut out and tapes to toothpicks and stuck to the battlements with a piece of PlayDoh. The client and therapist then enact the battle. The therapist will say one of the externalized negative self-talk statements while pretending to fire the tank. The client must defend his fortress by saying his positive replacement thought out-loud while pretending to destroy the enemy.

Processing Questions:
What are some of the weapons (statements) the enemy used to try and defeat you?
How did you see the danger coming?
What weapons (statements) did you use to defend your territory from the enemy?
How can you do this same kind of thing at school or at home without the fortress in front of you?

Homework Assignment:
Have the client make a list of the most troubling one or two negative self-talk statements as they were identified in the game. Have the client take home the "banners" with the counter statements written on them. Ask the client to practice thought stopping and thought replacement each time the negative self-talk statement comes into his head.

Special Considerations:
It is important that the client be able to own the positive self-talk statements that are crafted. The therapist can create many restructured cognitions, but if the client can't believe them enough to practice them, he will never take ownership of them. Make sure the client can accept the restructured statements he helps to create.

Applications and Modifications:
This technique can be applied to any number of disorders that are helped by Cognitive-Behavioral treatments, including Anxiety Disorders, Depressive Disorders, Obsessive-Compulsive Disorder and faulty belief systems that have emerged in a client through traumatic experiences.

© Paris Goodyear-Brown, 2005. All Rights Reserved.

Put a Positive Spin on It

Treatment Modality: Individual/Group/Family
Population: Ages 7 and up
Treatment Phase: Working phase

Treatment Goals:
1. To educate the client about CBT
2. To identify negative thought patterns
3. To restructure problematic cognitions
4. To practice replacement statements

Props:
Various spinning tops
Butcher paper or large construction paper
Markers

Procedure:
This technique is another useful tool to help teach child clients the basics of thought restructuring. The three primary cognitive distortions, according to Aaron Beck, are the following:
1) I am inadequate
2) The world is unjust
3) The future is hopeless

More than likely, if you are dealing with a child who is suffering from depression, anxiety, etc., this child is caught somewhere in this cognitive triad. Our job as clinicians is to help our clients replace these distortions with self-talk that will create hope and positively impact resiliency.

It is important to have three "sets" of two tops on hand when doing this exercise. The two tops in each set should "match" in size or shape, but differ in color or decoration. For example, two wooden tops, one blue and one green could be a set. Each set will correspond to each of the cognitive distortions mentioned above. Let the child choose one set of tops to begin. Say to the child, "I've been thinking about how much you've been worrying and I'm remembering some of the other kids I see (normalization, universalization) who worry. They tell me that their brains say that they are no good, stupid, and that they can't do things right (inadequate is a word that one might use with an articulate adolescent, but will need to be replaced with age appropriate language for younger children). Help the client exhaust the list of negative self-talk statements that contribute to this root belief "I am inadequate". Have the child write these down as they come up on various parts of the butcher paper. Give the child one top and have him spin it on the butcher paper. When the top lands on one of the faulty cognitions, have the child draw a picture or face of the resulting feeling that comes after they think these thoughts. Part of the fun is choosing which statement you want the top to land on and then spinning it to try and make it land there. The child will do this over and over again if you have a wide variety of tops.

The second part of the intervention builds on the first. Help the child craft positive replacement thoughts for the "I am inadequate" statements. Have the child write these on a separate piece of butcher paper (it helps if this paper is a lighter, brighter color than the first). The second top is then introduced and the child gets to spin it. As this top lands on various restructured thoughts, the client adds a feeling face or other picture that this new thought engenders. This process can be repeated over several sessions while working through Beck's cognitive triad.

© Paris Goodyear-Brown, 2005. All Rights Reserved.

Processing Questions:
How did it feel (on a scale of one to ten) to write the thought, "I am no good"?
When you spun the top on the first paper, it could only land on a thought that makes you feel bad. How did you change this?
How did it feel (on a scale of one to ten) to write the new thought, "I am good at many things"? (Insert whatever thought the child crafted.)
How can you practice replacing one with the other?

Homework Assignment:
Give the child a small top to take home with them. Instruct him to carry the top in his pocket as he goes to and from school and other events. As the child begins to have one of those old thoughts come up, the child should hold the top in his hand and imagine spinning it. If it will not be distracting, the child may even take the top out and spin it as he practices thinking the replacement statement. Parents can be asked to reward the client whenever they see the child using the top to practice the new thoughts. The parent and child can design a pie chart with rewards listed on it. The child can spin the top and receive whatever reward the top lands on.

Special Considerations:
Part of the motivation to engage in the hard work of cognitive restructuring is the novelty of spinning the tops and watching them fall on the written statements. Therefore, it will be important to have a variety of tops to which children will be drawn. Another important consideration is tied to Beck's cognitive triad itself. Through initial assessment, you will find that the child is most mired in one of the three cognitions targeted in the triad. Therefore, the bulk of your work may be focused at restructuring a primary faulty cognition. You will want to begin the "game" with the one that is most problematic

for your unique client, as the novelty or motivation may wear off after the first set of reframes is completed.

Applications and Modifications:

This activity is particularly conducive to a group setting. A large piece of butcher paper can be used and each group member gets to write down one or two negative thoughts related to one part of the triad. Each client then gets a turn to spin the top and see where it lands. This technique can also be done in families. This can be a powerful exercise in families, as negative generational patterns of thought can be exposed and modified.

Cognitive-Behavioral Play Therapy Techniques

Punching Holes in that Theory

Treatment Modality: Individual/Group/Family
Population: Ages 6 to 18
Treatment Phase: Working Phase

Treatment Goals:
1. To help traumatized clients articulate lies told to them by their perpetrators
2. To explore any internalization of these lies as false beliefs
3. To confront and reconstruct these thoughts

Props:
Construction paper
Markers
Hole punchers (in various shapes)

Procedure:
Children who have been traumatized can have complex belief systems related to the trauma. Children who have been physically or sexually abused, for example, may have a number of beliefs that stem directly from lies told by the perpetrator of the abuse. Perpetrators often attempt to place the blame or "fault" for the perpetration on the person of the victim. Victims will often accept the blame and thereby internalize the belief that they are responsible for the abuse. This activity will allow the child to articulate a false belief engendered by the

perpetration situation. Trust and healthy rapport must be present between the client and the therapist before a client will be able to engage in this sort of exploration.

Cut up strips of construction paper in the shape of cartoon thought bubbles. Begin by asking the client to repeat any statements that she remembers the perpetrator making related to blame. Talk with the client about how they may have taken these statements in as "the truth". Have clients write down each of the false belief statements in the thought bubbles. Then introduce the hole punchers. Model for the client how to punch a hole in paper and then allow the client to have two or three practice turns. Explain to the client that she will get to a punch a hole in the statement she wrote down as she verbalizes a counter-statement. For example, if the client wrote down "I made it happen because I wore a short skirt that day," the client will make counter statements such as "I am not responsible for what happened" or "Lots of girls wear short skirts and don't get hurt, so that can't be the reason" while they punch holes in the written false belief. Clients are more likely to spend time countering the false belief if various shapes of hole punchers are available. Hole punchers in the shape of stars, hearts, hands and other icons can be purchased at craft stores. By the end of the activity, there should be so many holes in the written false belief that it can no longer be read. A full body adaptation of this technique would be to write the lies on large butcher paper, hold it up and let the client physically punch through it while verbalizing "the truth".

Processing Questions:
What did the person who hurt you say about why this was happening to you?
Do you believe that you are responsible for what happened? What makes you think this?
What can you say to yourself to place the blame back where it belongs?

© Paris Goodyear-Brown, 2005. All Rights Reserved.

Homework Assignment:
Explain to the client that other false beliefs related to the trauma may come up over the course of the week. As they do, the client should be invited to write them down. The client can engage in debunking the false belief at home using a pencil or her own hole punch to punch holes in the theory.

Special Considerations:
Clients may have great difficulty letting go of feelings of responsibility related to the abuse. Education regarding typical thought processes of survivors of abuse will be beneficial in helping clients shift cognitive distortions. Young children will not find the written word to be helpful. The activity can be shifted in this population to give the client an experience of empowerment and control over the perpetrator. Invite the client to draw a picture of the perpetrator. Invite the client to make whatever verbalizations will make them feel strong (this might be "shut up", "You're a liar", "I hate you", "Go away", etc.) as she punches holes in the image of the perpetrator. When enough holes have been punched, the perpetrator's image should be virtually unrecognizable.

Applications and Modifications:
This technique can be used as a teaching tool for groups of traumatized children. In this milieu, a "perpetrator" body can be drawn and cut out by the group. The group can generate lies that are commonly told by perpetrators and these can be written on the body of the perpetrator symbol. Group members take turns confronting and debunking these lies out loud as they punch holes in the perpetrator's comments.

© Paris Goodyear-Brown, 2005. All Rights Reserved.

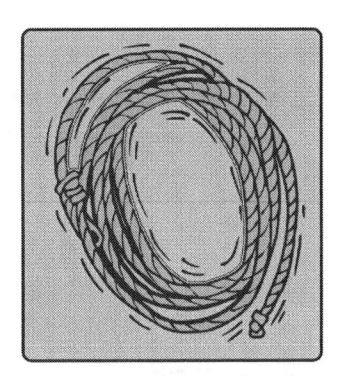

Lasso the Loser

Treatment Modality: Individual/Group/Family
Population: Ages 3 to 18
Treatment Phase: Working phase

Treatment Goals:
1. To identify the client's faulty beliefs
2. To combat the client's belief that the abuse was his fault
3. To empower the client to assign blame to the perpetrator
4. To give the client a kinesthetic experience of removing the perpetrator

Props:
Sandtray
Miniatures
Red or black licorice strings

Procedure:
Begin by introducing the empty sandtray to the client. Invite the client to create a world in the sand that shows "the abuse". This is a directive sandtray prompt. Phrase the prompt in whatever terms the client has used. If the client has talked about the secret, say "Show me the secret in the sand", If the client talks about it as the bad thing that happened, say "Put all the people involved in the bad thing in the tray". Then

encourage the client to take you through the sandtray. Some children will need many prompts like "What happened first? What happened next?" Other children will be uncomfortable with this kind of processing, in which case you move on to the next step. Next, introduce the container of strawberry licorice. Food is one of the many ways that we nurture children and it works as a good motivator to let the child know that when the activity is over, that she may have a piece of the licorice for herself. Take one string of the strawberry licorice and make a lasso out of it. Then, while looking directly at the tray, ask the client "Who is the loser in this tray?" The client may very well begin by pinpointing herself. The client may display a faulty belief that she was responsible for what happened. Confront the faulty belief. Continue confronting it until the client is able to shift the blame to another in the tray. When the client is ready, give her the licorice lasso. Invite her to "lasso the loser" and pull another miniature out of the tray. Then process what the tray feels like with this character removed. Depending on the child's needs, you may decide to cage or contain the perpetrator in some other place in the playroom, away from the sandtray.

Processing Questions:
In the tray, show me what happened to you.
Describe each character. How do you feel about each one?
What's it like for the characters in this world?
Who is the loser in this tray?
Who would you like to remove?
How does the tray feel now without that character?

Homework Assignment:
Have the client visualize the perpetrator being whisked away from the scene with a lasso. Ask the client to visualize this image whenever thoughts of the perpetrator start to be overwhelming.

© Paris Goodyear-Brown, 2005. All Rights Reserved.

Special Considerations:
Self-blame can be difficult to impact. It may be beneficial to have the client treat the miniatures in the tray like characters in a story. This allows the client to maintain some distance and perhaps see what happened (and who's to blame) from an outsider's perspective.

Applications and Modifications:
This technique can be used in family therapy when a protective parent is available to be there. The clients could co-construct the tray and can help each other confront their faulty beliefs. Parents may be suprised at how much self-blame a child has internalized. It can be very healing for the child to hear directly from the parent that it is the perpetrator and not the child who is to be held responsible.

The Why Wheel

Treatment Modality: Individual/Group/Family
Population: Ages 6 to 18
Treatment Phase: Working phase

Treatment Goals:
1. To exhaust the list of attribution about why a traumatic event happened
2. To challenge the attributions that would lead to self-blame
3. To discard the attributions that are associated with false beliefs

Props:
Template of a question mark
Construction paper or poster paper (thicker papers are better for this activity)
Scissors
Markers
Mini trash can

© Paris Goodyear-Brown, 2005. All Rights Reserved.

Procedure:

Most survivors of trauma have some faulty beliefs about the cause of the trauma. In no case is this more true than with young children. Children engage in magical thinking and often jump immediately to the assumption that it is their fault when bad things happen. If a child is angry with his mother and she gets hurt in a car accident, the child assumes that he caused it by his anger. A pre-pubescent girl is sexually abused by a friend of the family and she believes that she caused it by being attractive or wearing certain kinds of clothes. It is critical that our clients examine their attributions in order to avoid self-blame, self-hatred, and other related negative feeling states.

In this activity, begin by showing the client the template of the question mark. Explain to him that you are going to make a "why wheel" to try and answer the question "Why did this bad thing happen?" Most children love to cut things out and adolescents will be relieved that this activity keeps them from having to make constant eye contact with the therapist. Help the client trace and cut out at least ten question marks. When this is completed, ask the client to tell you all the reasons why he believes the bad thing happened to him. If the child is old enough to write, have him write each attribution on one of the question marks. As the list is being generated, have the client hang the next completed question mark from the crook of the previous question mark (this will resemble Monkeys in a Barrel). As the chain of question marks gets long enough the last question mark can be hooked back to the first and the whole series become a circle. The circle (or chain necklace) can then be hung around the client's neck. Talk to the client about the burden involved with carrying around all these beliefs about why this thing happened. Then go through the question marks one by one with the client. Challenge any attributions that are grounded in a faulty belief system. Once the child is willing to discard this reason, have him rip the question mark in two and throw it in the waste basket. In this way, help the client work through all of the attributions that lead to self-blame or false responsibility.

Processing Questions:
Why do you think the bad thing happened?
What is one reason that you think the bad thing happened but you've been too afraid to say out loud?
Why else do you think it happened? (Continue questioning until the client's list of attributions is exhausted.)

Homework Assignment:
Ask the client to notice each time during the following week when one of these faulty answers to the "why" question comes into his head. Have him keep a tally of them. During the next session he can focus on rational responses to the most troubling self-blaming "whys".

Special Considerations:
A very important part of healing for children who have been traumatized is related to placing the responsibility for the abuse in the correct place. Self-blaming cognitions must be examined and discarded. This is one activity aimed at bringing the self-blaming statements to the client's awareness. It may be difficult for the client to realize the irrationality of his self-blame and the therapist must take an active role in confronting the faulty thought patterns. It is also important that the client have replacement statements or cognitions that counter the effects of the self-blaming mantras. This technique is best suited to the working phase of treatment because the role of the therapist is to help challenge unhealthy beliefs and this requires that trust and rapport be pre-existing.

Applications and Modifications:

This technique could easily be modified for a group setting. Groups of survivors of sexual abuse or domestic violence are invaluable because they normalize and universalize the response that children often have to these unique traumas. Doing the "Why Wheel" in the group setting would allow for each group participant to see that others have the same self-blaming attributions in which he is mired. As each distorted attribution is dealt with and destroyed all group members benefit.

Thinking Caps

Treatment Modality: Individual/Group/Family
Population: Ages 6 to 18
Treatment Phase: Working Phase

Treatment Goals:
1. To increase positive self-esteem
2. To identify negative self-talk statements
3. To generate positive self-talk statements
4. To practice thought-stopping and replacement strategies

Props:
Two different color plain caps
Permanent markers (various colors)

Procedure:
Children often have a difficult time recognizing that they can control their thought life. Children need education about how their thoughts effect their feelings and behaviors. This process is complicated by the fact that thoughts are abstract entities.

They are generated in the brain, but are not touchable like fingers or toes. Transferring the thought life to "thinking caps" allows for the client to externalize and to some extent concretize her thoughts. These externalized thoughts can then be manipulated, restructured and transformed into more helpful cognitive constructions. It is useful to have a series of blank caps available to the client (these can be purchased inexpensively in bulk through mail order catalogs).

Begin by taking one cap and dividing it into sections by creating lines on the hat with permanent marker. Give the client examples of negative self-talk. "I can't do anything right", "I'll never have friends", or "nothing will ever change." Ask the client to repeat one of these statements that relates to her own thought life. Have the client rate how this statement makes him feel on a scale from 1-10. Have the client write the negative self-talk statement in one of the sections of the cap. The client may also want to write down the number that reflects the feeling engendered by the statement. Have the client generate as many negative thoughts as possible, writing one in each section of the hat. Statements may need to be written on the bill of the cap and even on the inside. The first cap becomes the reference point for the creation of new, positive self-talk statements. Give the client a second cap that has also been marked into identical sections. Taking each negative thought in turn, help the client generate a replacement statement. Have the client practice saying this new thought out loud while they write it on the new cap. Have the client rate how she feels after saying this new thought to herself on the same scale she used to measure his feelings response to the negative thoughts. Invite the client to label each cap. One may be called "dark thoughts" and one called "happy thoughts". One may be called "stuck thoughts" and the other "new thoughts". Let the child choose the names, as long as she clearly delineates one of the caps and the thoughts recorded on it as preferable to the other one. Then, take the client through a series of role plays. Create situations that mirror real life situations for the client. Have her respond to the situation

© Paris Goodyear-Brown, 2005. All Rights Reserved.

wearing her first thinking cap. Then have her switch hats and respond differently based on the second thinking cap. This activity allows the client to feel a sense of empowerment. She can literally control which thoughts she chooses to think by physically switching the hats. As she practices this process, she will become more and more proficient at quickly identifying and restructuring negative self-talk in other life arenas.

Processing Questions:
What are some thoughts that you think that make you feel bad?
What could you say to yourself instead to feel better?
Who is in control of what you think?
How can you recognize that you are thinking something negative?
How do you change your thoughts?

Homework Assignment:
If the parent has not been conjointly involved in the activity, invite him in at the end of the session. Have the client describe the activity and the two caps in her own words. Lead the client and parent through a role play that allows the client to wear both hats. Ask the pair to play this same game at least one time a day between sessions.

Special Considerations:
Children do need to be able to read and write to benefit from this activity as it is described. However, with preschool age children, there could be a one to one correspondence between caps and thoughts. On one cap the child could draw a picture of herself thinking she's stupid. On a second cap, the child could draw a picture of herself riding a bike or doing some other activity that proves she is not stupid, but that she is indeed competent. The client puts on the first cap and makes a face to show how she feels when he thinks about being stupid.

The client puts on the second cap and makes a face to show how she feels about being able to do the activity drawn on the cap.

Applications and Modifications:

The thinking cap exercise can be easily adapted to address negative self-talk components of different diagnoses. A diagnosis specific set of cognitions can be targeted, challenged and restructured using the thinking caps. The thinking cap can also be used to help children who suffer from nightmares. Children frequently say, "I can't stop the bad dreams/thoughts/etc. from getting into my head". For these clients, one cap can be created to act like a force field around the client's brain. The clinician helps to fill the sections of this cap with soothing statements, strategies, descriptions, and images of happy places and sweet dreams. The client and caregiver go over all the things written on the cap before bedtime and the client wears the hat to bed.

© Paris Goodyear-Brown, 2005. All Rights Reserved.

Erase the Place

Treatment Modality: Individual/ Group/ Family
Population: Ages 4 to adult
Treatment Phase: Working Phase

Treatment Goals:
1. To pinpoint cognitive distortions based on negative messages sent by others
2. To refute these negative messages
3. To combine kinesthetic expression with verbalization of cognitive counter-statements in order to displace the original negative message

Props:
White paper
Pencils
Erasers (an assortment)

Procedure:
This is a simple yet powerful activity that allows clients to address cognitive distortions that they have believed based on negative messages sent by others. This technique is versatile enough to be used with clients who are coming to treatment primarily for help with self-esteem as well as by those who are

coming primarily for help with trauma-based symptomatology. If the client can identify a perpetrator, the exercise can be framed in terms of the "lies told by the perpetrator". For example, a perpetrator may have told a child that the child was sexually abused because "she was bad". The client may have taken this in and created a cognitive distortion based on this lie from the perpetrator.

In this case, the client writes down the words said by the perpetrator as accurately as she can remember them. The lie is written in pencil on a white piece of paper. Then ask the client to tell you what they would like to say to refute the lie. The child may create a statement like, "I am good. You are bad." The child might just want to say, "Liar, liar, liar". Whatever verbalization the child wishes to make is O.K. The goal is not so much to re-train the client's cognitive process at this time. Rather, the goal is to give the client an experience of eradicating the negative message, thereby giving the client an experience of empowerment. The client is then invited to choose an eraser. It is more fun for the child if the therapist has a multitude of erasers in different shapes and sizes. Even giant erasers can be bought and added to the mix. The client is instructed to erase the statement written on the page while making the verbalization that they have previously chosen. The child will be scrubbing hard at the paper with the eraser while saying, "You're a liar. I don't have to listen to you anymore!!" The kinesthetic activity combined with the verbalization allows for both the visceral and cognitive engagement to happen simultaneously. The child should be encouraged to continue erasing and repeating the verbalization until all traces of the original message are gone. Some children end up scrubbing a hole through the paper in order to erase the negative message.

Processing Questions:

What is one lie that the person who hurt you told you?
Tell me one thing that you've heard from someone else that makes you feel bad about yourself.

What would you like to say to that person now?
How did it feel to erase the lie/ hurtful words?

Homework Assignment:
Explain to the client that the process of truly erasing the negative messages sent by others may take some practice. Instruct the child to watch out for that lie when it comes into her head. Ask her to again write it down and do the same erasing/verbalization exercise at home. Let her choose an eraser to take home and keep for just this purpose.

Special Considerations:
The hardest part of this exercise may be helping the client to generate the original negative message. Children take in and take on ownership of the negative messages they receive from others. "You're worthless" becomes "I'm worthless". The internal voice may have taken over so quickly that the client can no longer externalize it.

Applications and Modifications:
This activity can be modified for use with any number of diagnoses. The client can pinpoint her own cognitive distortions as they relate to depression, anxiety, etc. The main difference is in crafting rational responses that the client can verbalize while erasing the original negative self-talk, as opposed to making whatever confrontive verbalization the traumatized child makes to refute the lies of a perpetrator.

Clearing the Clouds Away

Treatment Modality: Individual/Group
Population: Ages 7 and up
Treatment Phase: Working phase

Treatment Goals:
1. To educate the client about the symptoms of depression
2. To identify the negative thoughts that may underpin the depression
3. To restructure problematic cognitions
4. To practice replacement statements

Props:
Cotton batting or foam
Gray spray paint
Paper
Markers
Yellow cellophane

Procedure:

This technique was crafted to give child clients a visual and kinesthetic way to represent and understand some of the concepts of cognitive-behavioral therapy as they apply to the diagnosis of depression. Many of our child clients have automatic thoughts and irrational beliefs, but they have not been able to articulate them. This activity helps the client to externalize thought life and then work to re-construct it.

Begin by having the client draw a large circle on a large piece of white paper as the therapist is drawing her own circle on her own paper. Tell the client that this represents the brain. Older clients, especially those with artistic talent, may wish to draw a more detailed model of the brain. The therapist then models the division of the brain into compartments that represent various thoughts. The therapist might begin by saying, " I'm good at being a friend," and drawing a line that sections off one part of the circle. Write the positive self-talk statement on the brain and tell the client how "good" this makes you feel. The therapist might say, "On a scale of one to ten, I feel like an 8 when I think this thought." Then take a piece of the yellow cellophane (or whatever other cheerful, see-through material is on hand) and overlay the thought with the cellophane. Have the client generate a positive self statement and follow the same procedure on his own paper. The therapist might then say, "But sometimes my brain says to me, "You're not very smart!" At those times, I feel like a 2 on our scale. It's almost like there is a cloud over my brain. (Cut the foam into cloud shapes before the client arrives). Draw another line sectioning off another part of the "brain". Write the negative self-talk statement on the cloud and attach it to the paper. Ask the client to follow the same procedure. Encourage the client to generate as many of the clouds as they can. Restructuring the cognitions may take several sessions, but it is important that she exhaust the attributions.

Once the clouds have been attached to the "brain", lead the client into a discussion of whether or not these thoughts are the "real brain". The "real brain" is the blank white paper underneath each of the clouds. Client and therapist can then methodically begin to take each problematic cognition (cloud) and restructure it. The restructured cognition or positive self-talk statement is then written on the white paper under the cloud. The resulting product can then be used as a goal chart. The client can permanently remove each cloud (revealing the positive self-statement underneath) as her brain is retrained. By the end of treatment, most if not all of the clouds will have been removed. Upon termination, the client can take the "healthy brain" home with her as a visual coach to prompt her to continue using the replacement language.

Processing Questions:

What is one thing you tell yourself that makes you feel bad?
On a scale of one to ten, (one being awful and ten being the happiest you've ever felt), how do you feel as you are thinking this thought?
Do you have any control over the thoughts you think? How?
What is one thing you could say to yourself instead (of the negative thought) that will help you feel better about yourself?

Homework Assignment:

Ask the client to choose one negative thought (one of their clouds) and try to become aware of how many times they think this thought during the week. In what situations does this thought come up? Practice stopping the thought and replacing it with the new thought that was generated in session. For younger children, it would be most effective to spend the last few minutes of each session creating a mini-cloud to take home. On one side is the negative thought, on the other side is the positive thought (or pictures). Giving the younger child one specific goal to work on increases the likelihood of completion.

© Paris Goodyear-Brown, 2005. All Rights Reserved.

Special Considerations:

Childhood depression may manifest as withdrawn, sulky, apathetic behavior or irritation, anger and aggressive behavior. It will be important to pinpoint the child's unique wiring and to help him or her find the pattern of negativity in his/her thought life as the activity begins. The therapist may end up using some confrontation to dispute the negative self-talk or the irrational beliefs. This can only be done after a relationship has been established and rapport has been built. The client must feel safe with the therapist in order for the child to allow the cognitions to be shaken. Also, part of the exercise that requires choosing a number on the "one to ten scale" may be easier for the child if they have a visual measure. For example, the therapist might create a thermometer of happiness and allow the child to point to the number or level after discussing each thought.

Applications and Modifications:

Teaching the concepts of cognitive-behavioral theory as it applies to the treatment of depression can be done in a group setting. However, as each client is likely to have idiosyncratic thoughts and beliefs that are tied to the depression, the activity is most effectively delivered in individual sessions.

Activities to Strengthen the Attachment Relationship

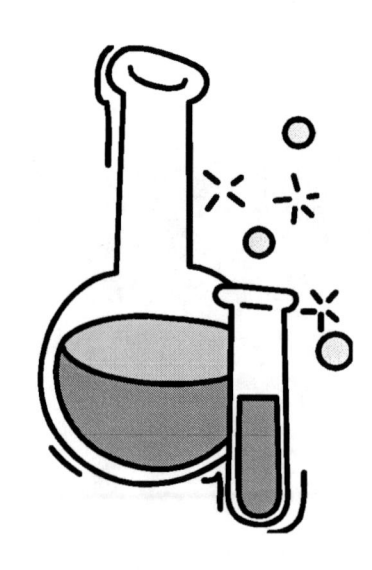

Sweet Dreams Lotion Potion

Treatment Modality: Family
Population: Ages 3 to 7
Treatment Phase: Working phase

Treatment Goals:
1. To give the client some control (at least in fantasy) over the bad dreams
2. To increase the client's sense of protection from the bad dreams
3. To increase relaxation at bed time through nurturing touch
4. To decrease both the intensity and frequency of nightmares

Props:
Lotions (of various colors and scents)
Bottles of various sizes, shapes and colors
Glitter
Mixing containers
Spoons or popsicle sticks
Mortar and pestle

Procedure:

Many young children suffer from nightmares. Some are induced by witnessing traumatic events. Some are the normal encoding of fears or emotionally laden experiences. All can be troublesome for both child and parent. Parents can feel helpless to rescue their child from repetitive nightmares. This particular intervention came out of a session with a five year old girl. During one of her first sessions, she reported having bad dreams about ghosts. I suggested a strategy for keeping the "scary pictures" out of her head. The little girl turned around, looked at me sadly and sighed. "Even if we helped my head, the bad dreams would come in through my foot." She went on to explain her belief that the dreams could get in through any part of her body. For this client, the dreams are a concrete problem and a solution must be presented in concrete terms. I said, "Sounds like we need a way to keep your whole body protected from those bad dreams." She nodded her head vigorously. This intervention came out of that conversation.

Present the child with a special tray or magical looking bag that is full of lotions. The lotions should have various scents and colors and should be in containers of various sizes and shapes. Explain to the child that these are the lotions from which a special Sweet Dreams Lotion Potion can be made. Each of the lotions has some magic in it, but when the lotions are mixed in the proper amount, the new potion becomes even more powerful. Direct the client to choose two or three lotions that seem to be the most powerful to that particular client. Some clients may prefer lotions with vanilla and cranberry scents. Others may feel the eucalyptus or ginger scents are more powerful. The child can always choose one favorite and just use that one. Have the client choose lotions that trigger happy and safe memories. Once the lotions are chosen, instruct the child to mix them in whatever quantities they desire to make their potion. The child can use spoons, popsicle sticks or other utensils to withdraw lotion from the original bottles. It

© Paris Goodyear-Brown, 2005. All Rights Reserved.

may be useful to collect sterilized meat trays or small plastic cups for mixing the lotions. It is important to have a clean disposable container for the new Sweet Dreams Lotion Potion, as the client will take this home. Clients may want to add glitter to make the lotion sparkle and thereby look more magical. The client may even wish to add dried flowers, etc. A mortar and pestle may be used to crush anything the child wishes to add to the lotion potion. After this step is complete, ask the caregiver to come into the room. Explain to the caregiver in front of the child (or let the child explain) that this Lotion Potion has special powers and when it is applied to the skin, it creates a magical shield so that the bad dreams cannot penetrate. Tell the child that the Sweet Dreams Lotion Potion works extra well when it is accompanied by singing. The parent and the child together can decide on what song to sing at bedtime. Instruct the parent to sing the song while applying the lotion to the child. Through this nightly activity, the child gets the power of the metaphor through the lotion, while being inundated with extra nurturing (through both touch and song) by the caregiver.

Processing Questions:
What does the lotion feel like?
What do you think of when you smell the lotion?
What song do you want to sing with your parent while she's putting on the lotion?
If you could speak to the nightmare, what would you say?

Homework Assignment:
Have a caregiver sing to the child while rubbing in the Sweet Dreams Lotion Potion each night before bed. Meanwhile, have the caregiver keep a nightly journal of the child's nightmares.

Special Considerations:

The most important consideration in this activity is the safety and reliability of the caregiver. The young child will see the nightmares as a concrete reality and so they need to be fought in concrete ways. The Lotion Potion gives the child a concrete way to fight the fear. However, the therapeutic value of this activity is multiplied when the caregiver can add nurturance to the nightly ritual. The soothing presence of the parent and the focused attention of rubbing in the lotion will have a double therapeutic effect. Since the effectiveness of this intervention rests on the nightly involvement of the parent, special care must be taken to help the parent buy into the theory underlying the technique.

Applications and Modifications:

This technique was originally designed to give preschool and elementary school aged children a concrete solution to the problem of nightmares. However, this technique could be modified to use with irrational beliefs or automatic thoughts. The parent and child could design positive statements to counter the irrational beliefs and aid in the cognitive restructuring process. This would be done in the office. Each night the parent could help rub in the lotion while both parent and child repeat the positive replacement thoughts.

Shaving with Dad

Treatment Modality: Family
Population: 3 and up
Treatment Phase: Working phase

Treatment Goals:
1. To give the child an experience of nurturing by his father
2. To encourage the father to give undivided attention and nurture to the child
3. To positively impact the attachment bond between father and son

Props:
Shaving cream (or whipped cream)
Tongue depressors
Plastic spoons
Smock
Towel
Bowl of water
Mirror

Procedure:

This technique is for use with families who are experiencing attachment difficulties. The research base on the importance of attachment relationships in early life to lifelong success or challenges in social relationships is clear. Many of the behavior problems that are prevalent in children seen in treatment stem directly from difficulties in their attachment history. Children who are securely attached have come to believe that their parents are "for them". They look to their parents for nurture, structure, protection, attunement, reflection of feeling states, soothing, teaching, and experiences of joy. Men raised in our independent American socio-cultural context may have had very few experiences of nurturing themselves. This creates challenges for these men when they become fathers and are thrown into a situation where continuous nurturing is required. This technique is one of several that I have created to help improve the relationship of fathers and sons. The idea is to re-create one of the male "rights of passage" between father and son in the playroom by learning to shave. It is important to explain the intervention (as well as a simplified version of attachment theory and its relevance to the family's healing process) to the father before the child is in the room. When the child enters, ask if he has ever seen his father shaving. Then explain that his father is going to teach him how to shave today. Explain that for safety, they will not be using real razors, but will get to pretend with popsicle sticks, spoons, or a safety razor.

First, the father shows the child how to apply shaving cream to his face, by beginning to apply some to his own. The father then asks the child to finish the job, so that it is the child who smooths shaving cream over the dad's face. The father then shows the child how to smooth the "razor" (popsicle stick) over his own face, and then lets the child finish the job. The roles are then reversed, and the child is invited to let the father "shave" him. The father would gently apply the shaving cream, all the while commenting on the wonderful face (eyes,

© Paris Goodyear-Brown, 2005. All Rights Reserved.

ears, nose, etc) of his little boy. Children love to have their physical bodies attended to by their parents. The father would then begin to "shave" off the cream. Young children delight in the idea that their face is "hiding" behind the shaving cream. The father can say things like, "Now where is Johnny's cheek...hmmm...I know it's under there somewhere...it's attached to his ear....(and as he swipes the shaving cream away)...here it is!!! The father can be encouraged to kiss the shaved places as they become shaved also. This is likely to transfer some shaving cream to the father's face, but this will add to the silliness and joy of the activity.

Processing Questions:
Ask each part of the dyad, in the presence of the other:
"How did the shaving cream feel on your face?"
"How did it feel to have your partner shave it off?"
"How easy or hard was it to trust that your partner would take care of you?"
"What was your favorite part of this game?"

Homework Assignment:
Have dad and son play this game at home one time during the week. It is often more powerful with the witness of another nurturing figure, such as a mother or grandmother, aunt or uncle. It is also a special treat to have someone videotape the game as it is played, so that father and son can watch it back together.

Special Considerations:
Part of the finesse that a therapist brings to the treatment process is knowing when to introduce a new intervention. This intervention is powerful in its intimacy, overt nurturing of each other's faces, and the focus on non-verbal dyadic communication. Families with extreme attachment difficulties may need to engage in other activities to push through the

initial animosity that may exist between father and son before this intervention is tried. Other activities that ease dyads into physical touch may be needed before this activity is introduced. Fathers especially may need to examine their cultural stereotypes and assumptions before trying this activity. Beginning clinicians should seek training and supervision in nurturing touch therapies before integrating a technique such as this one into their practices. Lastly, this technique is contraindicated for children whose fathers have ruptured attachments due to ongoing sexual abuse or extreme physical abuse.

Applications and Modifications:

Many of the families who come to treatment do not have a father actively engaged in the child's life. Sometimes abuse has been perpetrated and the father is now prohibited from contact with the child. Divorce, incarceration, relocation for job reasons, extreme mental illness, and even death are all reasons that a biological father may not be available. In these cases, an uncle, grandparent, or other trusted male in the child's life may volunteer to make up the other half of the dyad. If no one of this nature is available, a male therapist could engage in this dyadic work himself with the child. Appropriate training and supervision are needed before a male therapist should attempt to function as the nurturing agent in this intervention. Certain safety precautions would also apply, such as the express written consent of the child's primary caregiver and videotaping of all proceedings.

© Paris Goodyear-Brown, 2005. All Rights Reserved.

Meet in the Middle

Treatment Modality: Group/Family
Population: Ages 3 to 18
Treatment Phase: Working phase

Treatment Goals:
1. To give the client and caregiver an experience of nurturing
2. To give the client and caregiver an experience of mutual cooperation
3. To positively impact the attachment relationship between client and caregiver

Props:
Yarn
Ribbon
Silly String
Long strings of licorice

© Paris Goodyear-Brown, 2005. All Rights Reserved.

Procedure:

Families often come to treatment after the members have ceased to enjoy each other's company. One of the most important treatment goals at the beginning of work with such families is to give them experiences of enjoyment with each other. This activity is a stellar medium for increasing a parent and child's enjoyment of each other because it invites fun and spontaneity during the mutual completion of a task.

This activity is made up of a graduated series of tasks. The client begins with a task that requires mutual cooperation but is not overly intimate and ends in an activity that requires great intimacy between parent and child. Introduce the child and parent (they will be referred to as the dyad) to the following materials: yarn, ribbon, small fishing poles and canisters of silly string. Invite the child to choose the first material that will be used. Place one object from the playroom (perhaps a baby doll or a sandtray miniature) on the floor in the middle of the dyad. Explain that the goal of the game is to get the figure to a particular location in the room together. Each member of the dyad is given an end of a long piece of string, yarn, ribbon, etc. They may wrap the string around the figure, but otherwise are not allowed to touch the figure with their hands. Getting the figure off the floor while they both hold onto the ends of the string will require that they wrap the string around their own hands several times in order to make the string taut enough on both sides to lift the figure. In this way, a cooperative tug-of-war is set up. The parent and child will come closer to each other as they work on completing the task thereby bridging the distance between them as they wind up the excess string. When the parent and child have completed this activity there is a celebration.

The second activity literally takes out the middle man. This time the parent and child are given a long strand of licorice. Each is instructed to place his end of the licorice in his mouth. The goal of the game is to meet in the middle. Each person will chew up their piece of licorice until the two meet in the middle for a licorice kiss. This playful, nurturing intervention can give families a taste of the spontaneous fun they have been missing!

Processing Questions:
How did it feel to use the string instead of your hands?
What was it like to have to work together? What did you do well together? What can you work on?
How did it feel to finally move the figure?
What was the licorice game like?

Homework Assignment:
Have the parent and child play one version of this nurturing game each evening before bedtime between now and the next session. They may vary the cooperative material (yarn, ribbon, fishing wire instead of string) and the weight and size of the object to be moved.

Special Considerations:
The intervention may need to be adapted for various ages. For example, adolescents may love the challenge of negotiating the string to pick up and move an object, but be "too cool" to do the licorice kiss. Younger children might ask for the licorice kiss over and over again (after all, it combines sweets with intense nurturing attention from the parent), but have difficulty with the dexterity required to manipulate the string.

Applications and Modifications:
This technique lends itself well to a group setting. A group of parent/child dyads can complete the activities together. In fact, the gentle competition may increase the motivation of parent/child dyads in the group. Who will move their object first? Who will eat their licorice the fastest and meet in the middle for the kiss? The most important point, though, is that everyone will have fun!

© Paris Goodyear-Brown, 2005. All Rights Reserved.

The Toddler Tale

Treatment Modality: Individual/Group/Family
Population: Ages two to six
Treatment Phase: Working phase

Treatment Goals:
1. To improve the quality of the attachment relationship between parent and child
2. To equip the parent to build coherent narratives of life events for the client
3. To sequence and structure the details of important family moments

Props:
The child's body functions as the "book" in this exercise and is therefore the main prop
Large pen or marker

Procedure:
This is a wonderful activity to use with young children and their parents. One of the normal functions of the attachment relationship is that the parent acts as a structuring agent for the child. The parent helps the client process painful or

confusing experiences.   Often, when a child has an accident or has something scary happen, he will want to relay the story to his parent. Then, he will want his parent to tell him the story of what happened. He may urge the parent to tell other people the story of what happened. Indeed, when my own 3 year old had an accident that required a couple of stitches to his face, he had me retell the story to 11 different people over the course of a three day period. When a child has a parent provide structure and build a coherent narrative of a traumatic event, the child is able to inegrate the memory of the event into their own narrative more easily. The same process happens with warm, happy or silly memories. Parents in healthy families often tell stories about silly or cute things that their child did when he was younger. The child may roll his eyes at the telling, but he still grins and enjoys the family memory in which he plays an important role. He understands that he is a vital part of his family's identity.

    This exercise encourages the building of coherent narrative while increasing physical touch between parent and child. Begin by having the parent pinpoint a warm or funny memory shared with the child. Invite the child to lay down on the floor. The child lies on his left side with both arms out beside him. The parent pretends that the child's body is a book and his arms are the pages. The parent reads the front cover "The Day that Billy Ate Glue" by (insert parent's name). The parent then open the books by moving the child's top arm across his body, so that he is laying on his back with his arms open. The parent begins with the child's left arm and "reads" the story. For example, "Once upon a time, Billy Bates was sitting at the kitchen table making a picture. His mommy was making dinner, etc., etc., etc." The child's arms are moved back and forth as the pages are turned. As the final page is turned, the child's arms are placed back together as the child is turned on his other side. Then the parent announces "The End." Young children love this activity. They love listening to the story and pretending to be the book. They love having so much attention paid to their bodies. Once a fun memory has been processed

© Paris Goodyear-Brown, 2005. All Rights Reserved.

this way, the therapist may choose to move on to more difficult memories. Many "books" can be written this way in treatment. The child may wish to switch places with the parent and "read" his own version of a memory story.

Processing Questions:
How did it feel to be a book?
Tell me what you remember from the story.
What was the funniest part of the story? The silliest? The scariest?
Would you like to tell a story about another memory?

Homework Assignment:
Parent and child can be encouraged to play this game at bedtime. The parent will "read the book" of one thing that happened that day with the child.

Special Considerations:
Many parents (especially those who have themselves been traumatized) may need individual work in building their own coherent narratives before they are able to perform this function for their children. The therapist may want to have a practice session with the parent to make sure that the parent's memories of both fun and difficult events are coherent enough to be useful to the child.

Applications and Modifications:
This technique can be used to help families with young children process traumatic memories but it can also be used as a tool for reunification. When a parent has been separated from a child (perhaps through drug rehab, incarceration or temporary custody situations) this technique can help the parent and child focus on the attachment relationship that had been in place prior to the separation.

© Paris Goodyear-Brown, 2005. All Rights Reserved.

Powder Prints

Treatment Modality: Family/ Dyadic Work
Population: Ages 3 to adult
Treatment Phase: Working Phase

Treatment Goals:
1. To provide a positive, nurturing experience for child and caregiver
2. To encourage identification between child and caregiver
3. To encourage appropriate differentiation between parent and caregiver

Props:
Baby powder
Construction paper
Permanent markers

Procedure:
When dyadic communication deficits exist between a client and caregiver, underlying attachment difficulties may exist. This activity is a fun way to allow for the parent and child to engage

in a nurturing activity together. However, the exercise goes one step further in challenging the child and caregiver to articulate some of the ways in which they are similar to each other and some of the ways in which they are different. A mother/daughter dyad will be used in this example. Begin by asking mom to sprinkle baby powder into her daughter's hand. Have her rub the baby powder around. The baby powder throws the lines in the child's hand into stark relief. Ask the caregiver to look for as many shapes, letters, etc. as she can find in her daughter's hand. Each time she finds one, she says something like, "Wow...you have an "H" in your palm-see, it goes right through the middle." The mom can also write these down on the edge of her sheet of construction paper. When mom has exhausted the number of shapes and letters she can find, the daughter trades places with the mom. The daughter powders the mother's hand and the whole process is repeated. The daughter is likely to find some of the same shapes and letters as well as some different ones. This discovery is a great jumping off point for helping the mom and daughter embrace their similarities and their differences. Ask them both to put some more powder on their hands. Then each of them will place both hands on her own piece of medium to dark colored construction paper, leaving powder prints on the paper. In each finger of one hand, each of them writes down one way in which they are the same. These might be statements like, "We both have blonde hair," "we both love pizza" or "we're both afraid of snakes". On each finger of the other hand print, each of them writes one way in which she is different from the other. These might be statements like, "I like bike riding and she likes tennis", "She's shy and I'm not", etc.

Processing Questions:

What were some of the shapes that you saw in your partner's hand?
Which shapes did you both have? Which ones were unique?
What are some ways that you are like your mother (daughter)?

What are some ways that you are different from your mother (daughter)?

What is one way in which you wish you were more like your mom (daughter)? What's one way that you're glad to be different from your mom (daughter)

Homework Assignment:
Ask each client to do one thing between sessions to show appreciation for the differences between herself and her mother/daughter. This may be as simple as saying, "I'm really proud of you for working so hard on your piano lessons". For young children, it may be "Thank you for reading me books." In the next session, the clients can discuss any new awareness they may have about their similarities and differences.

Special Considerations:
The nurturing part of this activity is fun and beneficial even for the youngest child. Preschool age children may lose motivation quickly when the focus shifts to writing similarities and differences in the hands. Either the therapist needs to be actively engaged in scribing the child's ideas for her, or the child should be encouraged to draw pictures of the ways that she and mom are alike and different.

Applications and Modifications:
This exercise is useful with tramatized children, particularly those with abusive moms or dads. Latency age boys who come from domestic violence backgrounds will often begin to identify with their fathers by engaging in violent behaviors. This activity gives the client explicit permission to choose to be different from dad in some ways, rejecting the parts of dad's personality that the child does not wish to integrate into his own identity.

© Paris Goodyear-Brown, 2005. All Rights Reserved.

You're a Star!!

Treatment Modality: Family/Group
Population: Ages 4 to adult
Treatment Phase: Beginning/Working/Termination phase

Treatment Goals:
1. To equip family members with positive reinforcement as a behavioral modification tool
2. To increase appreciation between family or group members
3. To decrease attention to negative behavior
4. To impact the family culture towards support and encouragement

Props:
PlayDoh
Star cookie cutters
Star stickers
Star notebooks

Procedure:
Family therapy can be challenging, especially in the first few meetings with a new family. By the time a family has arrived

for treatment, family members are usually disillusioned with each other. There is little spontaneous positive affect and few nurturing exchanges between family members. One of the first treatment goals with these families is to positively change the family atmosphere or what could be called the "culture" of the family. Place the PlayDoh and a collection of star shaped cookie cutters on the table. Invite family members to begin cutting stars of different colors and sizes out of the PlayDoh. While family members are engaged in this activity, tell the family members that they are going to get to practice giving attention to behaviors that they like in the session. Have each one think of something another person in the family does that helps the family as a whole. These might be as simple as, "Thank you for making dinner for us" or "I like the way that you tuck me in at bedtime". This is a very safe starting activity for a family. The therapist makes it clear that negative comments or problems related to the family will be dealt with later, but that right now is a time to appreciate one thing about each other. Each family member creates a star for every other member present. Since the stars are made of PlayDoh, the client can carve the complimentary words into the star, carve a picture of the behavior into the star, or simply tell the person as the star is given to the person. After the PlayDoh activity is complete, process with the family how it felt to be appreciated by one another. Explain to the family that this "atmosphere of appreciation" will continue to be a part of the culture of therapy. Give each client a set of star stickers. Explain that as the family gets into the harder work of figuring out solutions to their problems, the stars will become even more important. As clients practice positive communication skills or engage in a positive behavior in the playroom, another family member can reach over and give the first a star sticker. The stickers can serve as a non-verbal appreciation without interrupting the flow of other activities or conversation.

Processing Questions:
How easy or difficult was it to think of a positive behavior for each family member? Why?
How did the other person respond when you told them about the behavior you appreciated?
What was one thing you liked hearing from another family member?

Homework Assignment:
Provide the family with a star-shaped notebook. Help the family decide on a place for their "Star Board" and explain that anytime someone in the family does something really helpful, any other family member can create a star describing the behavior and post it on the Star Board. All stars can be brought in to treatment each week for celebration.

Special Considerations:
Families may be so fixated on negative behaviors by the time they arrive for treatment that they try to phrase appreciative statements in terms that include previous negative behaviors, such as "Well, I'm glad that he finally cleaned up his room after weeks of me nagging him." The therapist's job is to point out the construction of the compliment and help the family member rework it until it is truly an appreciation statement.

Applications and Modifications:
This technique can also be a great aid to developing a supportive group culture. Unlike in family therapy, this activity should be saved for later in treatment when group members have had some experiences together. A "Star Board" can be created in the group space. Each group meeting can include a few minutes of time spent writing and sharing appreciation statements about other group members.

© Paris Goodyear-Brown, 2005. All Rights Reserved.

Termination Activities: Saying Goodbye

Bandage Banners

Treatment Modality: Individual
Population: Ages 4 to 15
Treatment Phase: Beginning/ Termination Phase

Treatment Goals:
1. To help clients identify the wounds caused by traumatic events
2. To establish treatment goals that will address these wounds
3. To increase the client's sense of empowerment related to the trauma
4. To celebrate the client's accomplishments during treatment

Props:
Toilet paper
Bandages
White strips of cloth
Markers
Sequins and other decorative craft items
A large person puppet or mummy doll (see picture)

Procedure:
Clients who come to treatment often need a safe place in which to explore the extent of the psychological injuries caused by trauma. Children are often more likely to discuss what has

happened to them if they are identifying with a character who has had similar difficulties. The identification symbol in my playroom is Michael the Mummy (see picture below). Mike is a very large stuffed doll covered in layers of cloth strips. A full sized child puppet who has also been covered with cloth strips could also be used. Have the wrapped puppet or mummy in a prominent location when the client enters the session.
Introduce the client to the mummy and explain that this mummy has had lots of hurts and has been wrapped up while the hurts heal. The client can be invited to guess how the mummy got hurt, but it is often more effective for the therapist to weave a story about the mummy's hurts that mirrors the clients own traumatization in some ways. For example, the therapist might say, "Mike's mommy and daddy used to fight a lot. They yelled a lot and it hurt Mike's ears-we covered them with bandages so they can heal. When we take them off his ears will feel better." The client may spontaneously begin to share details of his own domestic violence experience. If not, the therapist gets out the baskets of cloth strips, bandages, etc. and offers to wrap up the client. Once they have permission, many traumatized children take great pleasure in having their physical bodies attended to. Children often request band-aids, even for hurts that can't be seen. This activity takes that metaphor one step further. The therapist begins to wrap one of the client's arms while helping the client process one way in which they were hurt by the perpetrator. Perhaps the client is having nightmares now because of what happened. The therapist can wrap the bandage around the clients head to honor that hurt. The client or therapist then writes on the bandage a simple version of the treatment goal related to decreasing the nightmares. These bandages can be referred to throughout the treatment process as goals are revisited.
During termination, when many of the goals have been met, the client chooses clean bandages that will serve as banners. Have the client write coping skills, positive self-talk, and healing mantras on the strips. Invite the client to decorate them. During the final session, the therapist and client can pin them

up on the walls like crepe paper and they can serve as party decorations to help celebrate the client's graduation from treatment.

Processing Questions:
How has your body been hurt by the bad thing that happened to you? How has your mind been hurt? Your feelings? Your relationships? The way you see yourself?
What do you want to do about the hurts?
Imagine yourself all better. What would this look like?
How can we work on helping you feel better?
What are some things you learned in treatment that you can take home with you after we say goodbye?

Homework Assignment:
Tell the client that all the bandages can be left in the playroom. This gives the client the message that he doesn't have to carry all the hurt around with him all the time. The therapist will hold the hurts for him in the playroom. This functions as a psychological containment device for the client. Ask the client to spend the week thinking about which of the hurts he wants to start working on first. Next week, the original cloth strips are pulled out and one is chosen. Write the treatment goal related to this hurt on a new cloth strip. The client may choose to wear this during the session. Other interventions specific to the chosen treatment goal can then begin. At the end of treatment, the client is invited to take the new, decorated cloth strips home to hang in his room as reminders of his achievements in treatment.

Special Considerations:
Not all clients need to engage in the re-processing of their traumatic events. If a client is functioning fairly well he needs more interventions related to insulation, stress inoculation, and skill building. In this case, the clinician may choose to skip the

first step of the exercise. In other words, the clinician may create the first set of banners to reflect treatment goals without spending time beforehand on identifying the hurts. The rest of the delivery of this intervention remains the same.

Applications and Modifications:

This technique could function well in a group process. In a group of survivors of sexual abuse, for example, each member could create their own bandage describing one way in which he or she was hurt. The group as a whole could help each member design a treatment goal related to this hurt. At the end of the group process each group member can make his or her own achievement banner to take home. One nice addition to this exercise in a group format is that all the other group members can add encouraging statements, pictures etc. to each banner. When group members take their banners home, they will have a concrete reminder of the hard work they have achieved and the support of the group.

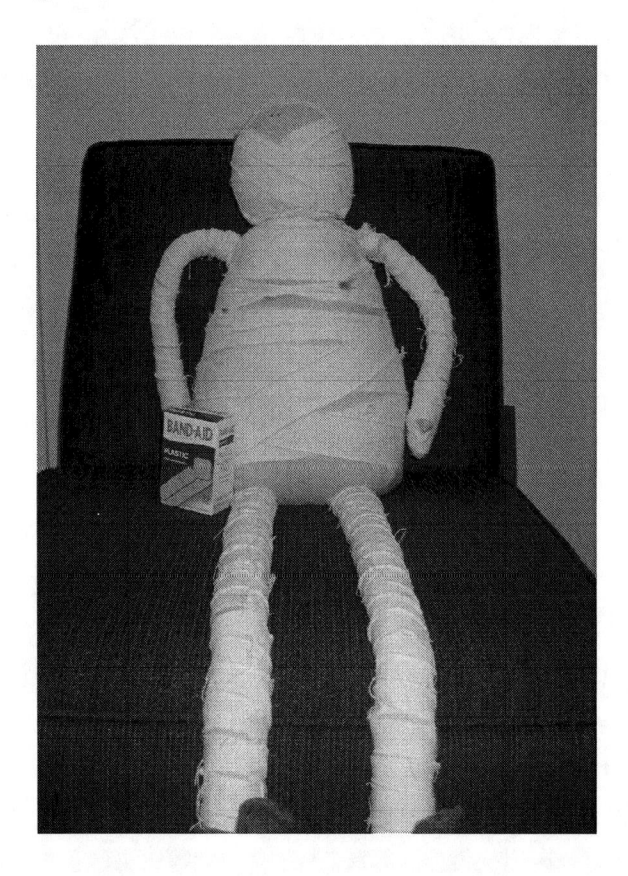

Calendar Collage

Treatment Modality: Individual/Group/Family
Population: Ages 4 to 18
Treatment Phase: Termination phase

Treatment Goals:
1. To structure the termination process for the client
2. To review meaningful events/ moments throughout the course of treatment
3. To create a concrete history of treatment that the client can keep as a link to the therapy experience

Props:
Poster/ construction paper
Magazines
Scissors
Glue

Procedure:
A critical piece of therapy with children and adolescents has to do with saying goodbye in a meaningful way. Creating a meaningful goodbye is an essential part of the treatment

© Paris Goodyear-Brown, 2005. All Rights Reserved.

process. Ironically, it is often the most difficult part of the process for child therapists. There are of sometimes countertransference issues involved that make it hard for the therapist to fully engage in the process of saying goodbye. This technique helps both the therapist and client honor the process. Whenever possible, therapists should give their clients at least four weeks notice that therapy is being terminated. In the best case scenario, termination becomes a celebration for the work done in treatment - a graduation of sorts. However, even if the termination is happening because the client or therapist is moving or the child is being placed in a home outside the area, four weeks should be given whenever possible. The client is likely to have four more sessions with a week in between each. When this is the case, a calendar collage can be a useful addition to the termination process.

Begin by drawing an accurate calendar of the days left until the client says her final goodbye to you, complete with dates and days of the week. Then invite the client to browse through the magazines, cutting out any pictures that remind the client of any part of the treatment process, the person of the therapist or her own life during treatment. The client might cut out a picture of a person crying because she cried in your office, or a picture of a basketball because this was one prop used in treatment. The therapist should also feel free to browse the magazines and cut out pictures to add to the collage. On each of the final four visits, the client chooses seven pictures and glues on in the calendar space for each day that has passed. This serves a double purpose, as it allows the client to see and enjoy visual images associated with memories of the therapy process while in effect counting down the days until the end of treatment.

Processing Questions:
What magazine pictures are you drawn to?
How does this picture remind you of our time together?
How does it feel to see all of these memories on the calendar?

© Paris Goodyear-Brown, 2005. All Rights Reserved.

Homework Assignment:
Ask the client to look at magazines at home as well and to bring in any pictures that she wants to add to the calendar. The client may have memories come up for which she cannot find a picture. Another homework assignment would be to have her draw pictures to add to the collage.

Special Considerations:
One temptation that may exist for both the client and the therapist at the end of treatment involves looking at treatment with "rose colored glasses". The client may only choose pictures that reflect the fun, the warmth, and the breakthroughs made in treatment. The therapist can give permission to remember the difficult times, conflicts, or confrontations between therapist and client by choosing pictures that touch on this content. The goodbye is more meaningful if the whole of the treatment processs is revisited instead of focusing just on the "warm fuzzies".

Applications and Modifications:
This technique is especially fruitful when done in a group setting. All clients involved in the group cut out pictures and then each shares his or her memories with the whole group. Each member of the group will have memories that are more salient for that member than for anyone else in the group, but sharing those memories enriches the narrative of the treatment process for everyone in the group. A collective calendar can be created or individuals may each make their own.

© Paris Goodyear-Brown, 2005. All Rights Reserved.

Graduation Gear

Treatment Modality: Individual/Group/Family
Population: Ages 3 to 18
Treatment Phase: Termination Phase

Treatment Goals:
1. To help the client revisit gains made during treatment
2. To honor the client for her hard work
3. To celebrate the client's achievements in therapy
4. To mark the leave-taking process for both client and therapist

Props:
Pieces of felt
Scissors
Yarn
Glue staples
Graduation robe
Certificates
Camera

Procedure:

From the *beginning* of a treatment *process* with a client, the therapist should always have in mind the goal of finishing well. It is the role of the therapist to help cast vision for the changes that a client can make in her own relationships, reactions, etc. Even when therapy is ended prematurely, a leave-taking ceremony that honors the client's work up to the point of termination can *be* performed. Children especially feel so proud of themselves when they "graduate" from treatment. The graduation process is a wonderful way to review the concepts that have been taught in treatment, the growth of the individual in various areas, and goals for future growth. Making the "accoutrements" of the graduation ceremony can *be* great fun and help the client prepare emotionally for the final goodbye.

Invite the client to make a graduation hat for the ceremony. Introduce several colors of felt from which the client can choose (lighter colors are better as the hat will have writing on it). Cut a square for the flat top of the hat and a long rectangle for the band of the hat. Write, or have the client write on the hat band the treatment goals that were addressed during therapy. Have the client write games played, concepts learned, symptoms reduced, etc. on the underside of the square. Finally, have the client write positive reflections about herself on the topside of the square. These may include such phrases as "I am a survivor" or "I never gave up" or "I can control myself now", etc. The hat band can then *be* glued, taped, or stapled to the square. Meanwhile, the therapist creates a graduation tassle out of several pieces of yarn. Each piece of yarn represents one positive quality or area of growth that the therapist has noticed in the client over the course of treatment. The therapist will share these verbally with the client and then attach the tassle. The therapist also completes an official looking certificate that says something like, "This certificate verifies that Jane Smith has hereby completed a course of play therapy on the 17th day of June, 2005. The client

© Paris Goodyear-Brown, 2005. All Rights Reserved.

and therapist both sign the certificate, as well as any caregiver who is present. Finally, the client dons the hat and the robe. The therapist makes an official kind of speech about all the client has accomplished. All important caregivers are invited to this ceremony. In fact, caregivers are invited to write letters describing the changes that they have seen in the client over the course of treatment. These letters can be read to the client during the graduation ceremony. If the client would like to have a picture of herself in the graduation garb and the legal custodian has given written permission, the therapist may photograph the client and give it to the client as a keepsake.

Processing Questions:
What are some of the goals that we worked on together?
What are some of your favorite games, activities or memories from treatment?
What are some things you learned in the playroom?
What do you want to keep working on after you leave treatment?
What are some things you are proud of related to treatment?
How does it feel to be graduating?

Homework Assignment:
As this activity will be completed in the last session or two of the treatment process, there is no homework assignment. Invite the client to keep the graduation hat and certificate in a place where she can see it and be reminded of the hard work she completed in treatment.

Special Considerations:
The youngest set of children, because of their developmental focus in the "here and now" may have difficulty with any sort of review of treatment. With this group of clients, the description of tasks accomplished and growth achieved will be largely the responsibility of the therapist and caregivers. It is important

to celebrate these children in an animated fashion, so that they have a sense of their own success.

Applications and Modifications:

This graduation process can be very special when completed with a family unit or in a group setting. Each family member creates his or her own graduation hat, but other family members can contribute to the positive growth statements on the top square of hat. In a group setting, each child can write something positive on the hat of every other child in the group. In this way, each client gets to keep a record not only of her own achievement, but of the recognition of this achievement by others who were on the journey.

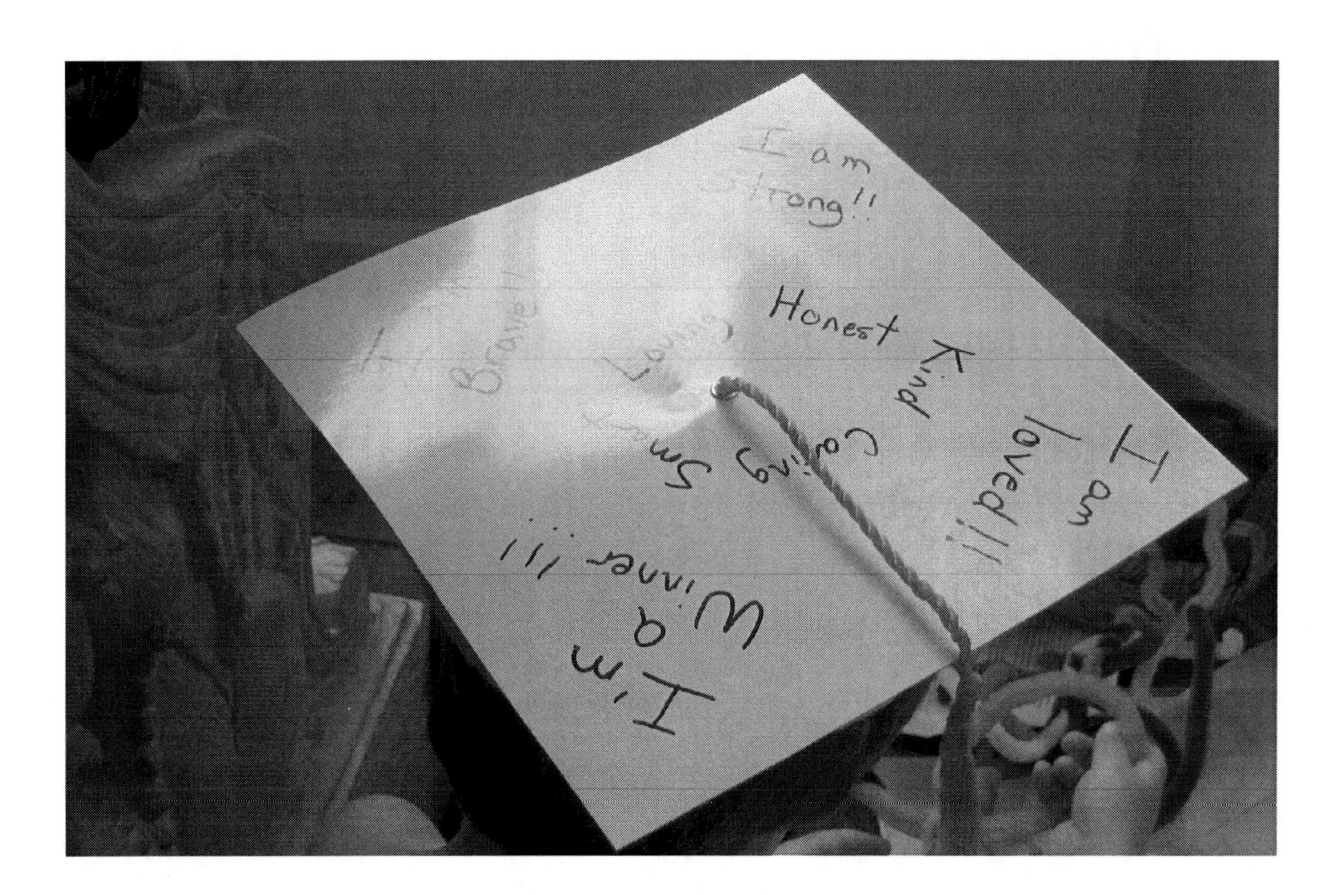

Pat on the Back

Treatment Modality: Group/Family
Population: Ages 4 to adult
Treatment Phase: Termination Phase

Treatment Goals:
1. To help clients revisit gains made during treatment
2. To utilize altruism in the group setting to help clients support each other
3. To celebrate the clients' achievements in therapy

Props:
Constuction paper or felt
Markers
Scissors
Masking tape

Procedure:
A pat on the back is usually given for a job well done. As clients near termination they often begin to have doubts about how much was actually accomplished in treatment. Clients will downplay or minimize their own treatment goals. Occasionally, child clients will revert to previous problematic behaviors as

termination approaches in an unconscious plea for continued relationship with the therapist. While this reaction may be understandable, it must be discouraged. One way to do this is to help highlight for clients the gains that they have made in treatment. When a client has been accompanied by others on their treatment journey (in group or family therapy) other people may see a client's growth more clearly than the client himself.

In this exercise, several colors of felt and construction paper are placed in the group space. Group or family members are paired up and trace the outline of each other's hands. Each member of the group should generate enough hands to be able to give at least one to each person. Clients can spend time cutting out the hands while the therapist explains what will happen. Ask if anyone knows what a "pat on the back" looks like. Ask for volunteers to role play patting someone on the back while the first volunteer compliments the second on a job well done. Give several examples, so that the clients understand that the pat on the back should be specific, "I have noticed that you are able to pay attention for longer now than you used to" as opposed to general praise such as "Good job!". Each client is to think about each other person in the group and write down a specific praise for this person on one of his cutout hands. As each hand is completed, the client tapes the hand cutout to the other person's back. Each group or family member should end up with several "pats on the back". When the exercise is completed, each person can take off his "pats" and read them. These make great keepsakes to help remind clients of the gains they have made in treatment.

Processing Questions:
What is a "pat on the back"?
What are some examples of specific praise?
What is one area in which each group member has grown?
How does it feel to receive your own pat on the back?

© Paris Goodyear-Brown, 2005. All Rights Reserved.

Homework Assignment:
Have the client repeat as many pats on the back as he can remember to his caregiver. Have him take the cut out hands home and pin them up in a prominent location. Encourage the client to practice giving other people verbal pats on the back. For very young children, ask the caregiver to read all the hands out loud to the child before bedtime every night for a week.

Special Considerations:
There is a subset of clients who are very uncomfortable with receiving praise of any kind. However, in this activity the praise is not given verbally, at least initially. Clients may choose not to read the cut out hands out loud to the group. Some clients may not wish to look at them at all while still in group. These clients should not be pushed, but can take the hands home with them to read at their leisure. Children who are too young to read or write may draw pictures or dictate their specific praise to the therapist.

Applications and Modifications:
This activity could be done with an individual client. In this case, two options are possible. The therapist could create all the hands and give the specific praise to the client. The other modification would be to have the client engage in self-analysis and pat themselves on the back for the growth areas that they are able to recognize in themselves.

Termination Take-Aways

Treatment Modality: Individual/Group/Family
Population: Ages 4 to adult
Treatment Phase: Termination phase

Treatment Goals:
1. To review treatment goals addressed during therapy
2. To help the client highlight positive changes made during treatment
3. To give the client a visual reminder of coping strategies learned during treatment

Props:
Chinese take away boxes (these can also be found in various colors and styles through mail order catalogues)

Procedure:
By the end of the treatment process, clients have attained mastery of certain strategies, behaviors, relational skills, etc. that were learned and practiced in the treatment process.

© Paris Goodyear-Brown, 2005. All Rights Reserved.

Children are often excited about their new found abilities, but also reluctant to leave the safety net of their visits to the therapist. This activity is aimed at helping the client articulate and celebrate her treatment gains. Begin by introducing the take-away boxes to the client. Traditional white boxes with red Chinese symbols can be used (and purchased cheaply from a local Chinese restaurant). Take-away style cardboard boxes can also be purchased from mail order novelty catalogues. These boxes come in a variety of colors and in specific designs (i.e. white hearts on a red box). Ask the client what these boxes are used for. The client will probably say that people take home leftover food in the boxes. Explain that even though the client's work in the playroom is coming to an end, there are many aspects of the work that she can take with her. The client is invited to draw pictures on the box that help her remember her time in the playroom. These pictures may include: 1) images of activities that the client and therapist completed together; 2) images representing skills learned in treatment or restructured cognitions; 3) images representing therapeutic achievements of which the client is proud; 4) written statements that function as mantras or self-soothing reminders for the child. The client then writes down statements that have been learned or practiced in session. "I am a survivor," "I can control my own behavior", "I am good at listening to others". These are written on small slips of paper and put inside the box. The therapist also writes down affirming statements about the client's positive change and growth during treatment. The activity is even more fun if the therapist has the facilities and time to help the client bake the positive statements into fortune cookies. The cookies are then wrapped, put in the box and taken home for the client to read and eat after termination.

Processing Questions:

What accomplishment are you most proud of related to your work in the playroom?

What is one way in which your behavior changed over the course of our time together?
What is one thing you learned about yourself in the playroom?
When you close your eyes and listen to my voice in your head, what do you hear me saying to you?

Homework Assignment:
The client gets to leave her final session with the take away box. Encourage the client to pull out the box and read through the statements inside whenever she begins to miss the therapist or faces new challenges in her life.

Special Considerations:
Clients particularly like to read the compliments, validations, etc. written by the therapist. Try to tailor written statements to each child's unique personality and the unique relationship between therapist and client. Children who are too young to read and write will rely heavily on parental involvement for the post-treatment ulitization of the take-away box. Bring the parent into session and have the parent read all the positive comments out loud once during the last session. Encourage the parent to take the initiative in pulling out the take away box and revisiting the written memorializations of the client's positive growth. This should be done once weekly at first.

Applications and Modifications:
This technique is a fun termination activity in group work. Each client in group is given her own take away box and decorates it with experiences of her time in group. All group members are encouraged to write about each other's positive growth in group, so that all group members are contributing to all other group members' take away boxes. Clients love to revisit the comments made by others after treatment has ended.

© Paris Goodyear-Brown, 2005. All Rights Reserved.

References and Resources

Ainsworth, M. D. S. (1967). *Infancy in Uganda: Infant care and the growth of love.* Baltimore: Johns Hopkins University Press.

Ainsworth, M. D. S. et al. (1978). *Patterns of Attachment: A psychological study of the strange situation.* Hillsdale, NJ: Erlbaum.

Bowlby, J. (1988). *A Secure Base.* New York: Basic Books.

Beck, A. et al. (1979). *Cognitive Therapy of Depression.* New York: Guilford.

Boyd-Webb, Nancy. (1991). *Play Therapy with Children in Crisis: A Casebook for Practitioners.* New York: Guilford Press.

Brazelton, T. B. & Cramer, B. G. (1990). *The earliest relationship.* New York: Addison-Wesley.

Brody, Viola. (1997). *The Dialogue of Touch: Developmental Play Therapy.* New Jersey: Jason Aronson.

Cassidy, J. (1994). "Emotion regulation: Influences of attachment relationships." In N. Fox (Ed.), *The development of emotion regulation. Monographs of the Society of Research in Child Development, vol. 59: 228-249.*

Emberley, E. (2002). *The Complete Funprint Drawing Book.* Boston: Little, Brown & Company.

Goodyear-Brown, Paris. (2003). *Gabby the Gecko.* Nashville: Sundog, Ltd.

Goodyear-Brown, Paris. (2002). *Digging for Buried Treasure: 52 Prop-Based Play Therapy Interventions for Treating the Problems of Childhood.* Nashville: Sundog, Ltd.

Harlow, H. F. (1962). " The development of affectional patterns in infant monkeys." In B. M. Foss (Eds.), *Determinants of infant behavior (Vol. 1, pp. 75-88).* New York: Wiley.

© Paris Goodyear-Brown, 2005. All Rights Reserved.

James, Beverly. (1989). *Treating Traumatized Children: New Insights and Creative Interventions*. New York: The Free Press.

Jongsma, A. E. et al. (Eds.) (2000). *The Child Psychotherapy Treatment Planner*. New York: John Wiley & Sons, Inc.

Kazdin, Alan E. and Weisz, John R. (2003). *Evidence-Based Psychotherapies for Children and Adolescents*. New York: Guilford Press.

Knell, S. (1993). *Cognitive-Behavioral Play Therapy*. New Jersey: Jason Aronson.

Levy, T. M. (Ed.). (2000). *Handbook of Attachment Interventions*. San Diego: Academic Press.

Nathan, Peter E. and Gorman, Jack M. (1998). *A Guide to Treatments that Work, 2nd Edition*. New York: Oxford University Press.

Osofsky, Joy D., (Ed.) (2004). *Young Children and Trauma: Intervention and Treatment*. New York: The Guilford Press.

Parr, T. (2001). *It's Okay to Be Different*. Boston: Little, Brown & Company.

Perry, B. D. et al. (1995). "Episodic memory and autonetic consciousness: developmental evidence and a theory of childhood amnesia." *Journal of Experimental Child Psychology, vol. 59: pp. 516-548.*

Rauch, S. L. et al. (1996). "A symptom provocation study of posttrauamtic stress disorder using positron emission tomography and script-driven imagery." *Archives of General Psychiatry, 53, 380-387.*

Rubin, P B. and Tregay, J. (1989). *Play With Them: Theraplay Groups in the Classroom*. Springfield, IL: Charles C Thomas Publisher.

Schacter, D. L. (1992). "Understanding implicit memory: A cognitive neuroscience approach." *American Psychologist, 47, 559-569*

Schacter, D. L. (1994). "Priming and multiple memory system: Perceptual mechanisms of implicit memory." In D. L. Schacter & E. Tulving (Eds.), *Memory systems* (pp. 233-268). Cambridge, MA: MIT Press.

Siegel, D.J. & Hartzell, M. (2003). <u>Parenting from the Inside Out: How a deeper self-understanding can help you raise children who thrive.</u> New York: Penguin Putnam.

Solomon, M. F. and Siegel, D. (Ed.) (2003). <u>Healing Trauma: attachment, mind, body, and brain.</u> New York: W.W. Norton & Company.

Sroufe, L. A. (1979). "The coherence of individual development." *American Psychologist, vol. 34: 834-841.*

Sroufe, L. A. (1996). <u>Emotional development: The organization of emotional life in the early years.</u> New York: Cambridge University Press.

Sweeney, Daniel S. and Homeyer, Linda E. (Eds.) (1999). <u>The Handbook of Group Play Therapy: How to Do it, How it Works, Whom it's Best for.</u> San Fransisco: Jossey-Bass, Inc.

Toth, S. L. & Cicchetti, D. (1998). "Remembering, forgetting, and the effects of trauma on memory: A developmental psychopathology perspective." *Development and Psychopathology, vol. 10, pp. 589-605.*

Vernon, A. (1993). <u>Developmental Assessment and Intervention with Children and Adolescents.</u> American Counseling Association.

<u>Websites through which resources can be purchased</u>:
www.childtherapytoys.com
www.constplay.com
www.orientaltrading.com
www.parisandme.com
www.playtherapy-toys.com
www.sandtrays.com
www.selfesteemshop.com
www.toysofthetrade.com
www.ustoy.com